Published by Grenadine Publishing 2011
Grenadine Publishing is an imprint of Massolit Publishing Ltd.

The Cocktail Book
© Stevali Production and Eliq Maranik 2011

First edition
ISBN: 978-1-908233-05-9

Product idea, cocktails and styling: Eliq Maranik
Graphic design and illustrations: Alan Maranik and Eliq Maranik / Stevali Production

Original title: Stora Cocktailboken
Translation by Rebecka Wolff / Stevali Production

All photos by Stevali Production, except:
p. 27–35 Maxxium
p. 41, 43, 45 Promotional photos from each restaurant
p. 36, 47 Helin Sepa
p. 26 Shutterstock
p. 6, 22, 40, 50, 54, 318 iStockphoto

Printed in Italy by Jeming Srl 2011

Grenadine Publishing
6 Artichoke Mews
Artichoke Place
London SE5 8TS
United Kingdom
www.grenadine.se

ELIQ MARANIK

THE
COCKTAIL
BOOK

250 RECIPES
COCKTAIL HISTORY
TRIVIA

Contents

250 COCKTAILS

'A pint, please ... as usual'

Are you the sort of person who always sticks to the usual pint or glass of wine in the bar? And, should you dare to venture into the cocktail menu, do you always order one of the old classics? If so, this is the book for you. The time has come to discover the world of cocktails out there just waiting for you, so let go of the bar counter and head into a jungle of flavours, colours, fruits, berries and glasses. The cocktails in this book are just as suitable for house parties as they are for formal dinners and other special occasions. *The Cocktail Book* does not simply offer you a great quantity of elegant drinks – everything from the well-known classics to more unusual and exciting varieties – it is also full of fun cocktail trivia to entertain your guests with.

Have you met the Collins family? Cocktails are not too different from people. They have a family, a past, and sometimes an interesting story that is just waiting to be told. Some have witty names while others have straightforward and logical ones. They all have their different qualities, some that you may like, and some that you may not like. However, you are now about to discover that the more you know about them, the more fun you will have mixing and drinking them. What does Mai Tai really mean? Was Bond's Martini actually shaken? And what is the difference between rum and Cachaça? And

that Hemingway fellow, what was it he said when he first tasted his new Daiquiri?

You are now holding everything you need in a systematic and concise format. The book explains all the terminology and all the functions of the bar equipment. You will learn about mixing techniques and be guided to legendary cocktail bars and places of interest worldwide.

When it comes to the origin of the word 'cocktail', there are probably as many explanations and myths as there are cocktails. Some are funny, like the one about the old unscrupulous bartender who would collect leftover spirits in a jug that looked like a rooster, and then sell the contents by the glass, 'tail for tail' to oblivious guests. Another bartender – a more generous one – used to serve his guests Coq au Vin and then use the colourful rooster feathers to decorate the drinks. Yet another theory claims that cocktail was a code word used to gain entrance to the speakeasies of the Prohibition era. No matter what story you choose to believe, the fact remains that the history of the cocktail, as well as of most cocktail recipes, offer interesting stories and fun facts – perfect for entertaining thirsty guests while preparing their drinks!

Eliq Maranik

Getting started

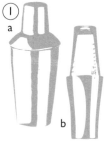

Equipment and Utensils

With the help of creativity, you can manage with whatever your kitchen has to offer. It is possible to shake Martinis in a clean glass jar and then pour the contents into cocktail glasses. However, you will find that it is both easier and more enjoyable to mix cocktails if you have the right equipment from the start.

Here is a list of the basic tools that will ease your path to perfect cocktails. Each piece of special equipment comes with a basic kitchen utensil at the end as an alternative.

The **shaker** is the bartender's best friend. It serves both to mix and chill the cocktails, quickly and efficiently. Always make sure that the shaker is at least half-filled with ice, and that you shake it with enough speed and vigour to prevent the ice from melting. When the metallic outer part of the shaker starts to get misty, the drink is ready to pour. This normally occurs after about 10 seconds of shaking. If you are using a plastic shaker, try counting '1 Mississippi, 2 Mississippi …' until you get to 10. No shaker at home? Try using a clean jam jar with a lid instead.

There are two types of shaker tins:

A *cobbler* (1a) consists of three parts and is easy to use. It looks a bit like a thermos flask and is made up of a tumbler, a lid with a built-in strainer and a cap. After shaking, simply open the lid and pour the drink as you would from a bottle – it will be strained automatically through the built-in strainer.

A *Boston shaker* (1b) is a favourite with professional bartenders. It consists of two overlapping parts. The bottom part is often a mixing glass and the upper is made of stainless steel. After shaking, tap the widest part of the gap between the sections. This will break the vacuum and loosen the glass. Strain the drink into a glass by opening the shaker just wide enough for the liquid to pass through, but for the ice to stay inside. Or open it fully and use a separate strainer.

A *mixing glass* (2) is used for cocktails that need stirring rather than shaking. Crystal clear cocktails are pretty to the eye, but a Manhattan, for example, becomes cloudy when shaken, which also goes for most drinks that include wine – red or white vermouth, sherry etc. Stirring a cocktail serves both to chill and to mix it. When mixing cocktails that are to be served without ice, including most short drinks served in cocktail glasses with a stem, cooling by stirring is vital.

The stirring technique involves filling the mixing glass to the brim with ice, pouring the ingredients on top (make sure the ice covers the liquid completely) and stirring. Stir 8–10 turns in either direction, and then up and down a few times, to ensure that the drink is properly chilled (remember to strain away the ice as quickly as possible afterwards, before it starts to melt).

The mixing glass is usually quite large and spacious, but if you have a Boston shaker at home you can use its glass part for stirring drinks instead. A jam jar will also do, even a pitcher or a jug – one with a spout is especially handy, and if it has a built-in strainer it is ideal.

If you have trouble fitting all your liquids inside the refrigerator, you can chill juices and other mixers before use by swiftly stirring them with ice in a mixing glass. The amount of ice in your glass is irrelevant; mixers at room temperature will quickly melt the ice and make the cocktail watery.

A **measuring glass** (3) is handy when trying to accomplish a perfect cocktail. Some cocktails are rather sensitive when it comes to the right proportions, and although professionals tend to achieve the right proportions by instinct, home bartenders may resort to the measuring glass as precaution. Short drinks and cocktails are extra sensitive when it comes in this respect, as they often contain a carefully measured balance between spirits and liqueurs. When making long drinks, the glass is often filled up with juices, carbonated drinks and other mixers, which makes them less sensitive to precision in measuring, which means there is room for creativity without running the risk of going 'wrong'.

Pour the different spirits in the measuring glass one at a time, not one on top of the other. You can use a jigger, which looks like an upside-down egg cup with a big cup at the one end and a smaller one at the other. The size varies with the smallest ranging from ½ oz (15 ml) to 2 oz (60 ml), depending on where in the world it has been manufactured. Alternatively, use the top of the cobbler, which resembles a one-ended jigger and holds 1–1 ½ oz (30–45 ml) liquid. This is a very handy utensil.

A **bar spoon** (4) is a spoon – about 25 cm (9,8 inches) long – for stirring drinks in a mixing glass. It reaches all the way down to the bottom of the glass and serves not only to stir the ingredients but also to move around the ice as much as possible in order to rapidly chill the drink. Some bar spoons have twisted handles. If you pour champagne along the handle you will prevent it from effervescing too much. Sometimes the spoon handle has a muddler at the end (read more about this tool below).

A **strainer,** sometimes called a **Hawthorn strainer** (5), is essential when pouring a stirred or mixed drink in order to prevent the ice from falling into the glass. It is made up of a perforated straining part and a removable coil that collects peel and seeds. The coil should fit the width of your mixing glass in such a way that the strainer forms a lid with the coil at the bottom.

A **muddler** (6) resembles a pestle. It is usually made of wood or some other relatively soft material. A muddler is used for crushing sugar, herbs, leaves and fruit in the drinking glass or mixing glass. Unlike a pestle, the muddler prevents the glass from cracking. A good muddler has one flat and one bulbous end. The flat one is ideal for fruit and the bulbous one is useful for crushing herbs. The flat end of some muddlers is uneven, which helps to release the flavours. Mojito is an example of a drink that is based on the muddling technique. Some bar spoons have a handle with a flat end that can be used for muddling.

A **blender** (7) is used for crushing ice, puréeing fruits and mixing frozen cocktails such as Frozen Margarita. A handy rule when it comes to making frozen cocktails is to allow the liquid to just about cover the ice in the blender – then the consistency will be perfect (what is perfect is of course a matter of taste; add the ice a little at the time and stop when the thickness is to your liking). Add the liquids first to avoid damaging the cutting blade. If you are crushing fruit for a fruit cocktail you can use a normal kitchen blender, but be careful when it comes to ice

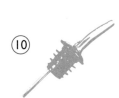

– both the blade and the motor can be damaged by big lumps of ice. Try crushing the ice into smaller pieces before putting it into the blender. A glass blender tends to last longer than one made of plastic.

A **juice extractor** (8) is a very handy tool. A small juice press can extract much more juice from a citrus fruit than squeezing a wedge between your fingers. A small, manual plastic reamer is fine for small amounts of juice, but if you plan to mix several cocktails at the same time, or make freshly squeezed juice at home, you may want to invest in an electric citrus juicer. Choose one that separates juice and pulp if you do not want to strain the juice after every pressing.

A **lemon zester** (9), or a **channel knife**, is very useful for peeling fine layers of zest from citrus fruits. It allows you to make long, curly twists of lemon or orange peel without accidentally getting some of the bitter white pith too. The twists can be used as flavour enhancers or decoration. You can, for example,

peel off a long piece and hang it over the rim of a glass.

Pouring spouts (10) are mainly used by pros, but are very useful for speed-pouring spirits in an even flow bartender-style while avoiding spilling and screwing caps on and off. Simply replace bottle caps with pouring spouts if you are having a party at home. There are different types, depending on the pouring-speed, as well as multi-functional spouts used for dripping or measuring liquor.

An **ice-crusher** (11), automatic or manual with a crank, is a good alternative to a rolling pin or hammer.

Cocktail sticks (12) are used for skewing cherries, lemon wedges, olives, fruits and berries and are just for show – you rarely eat the decorations. But they are nevertheless necessary; a fine cocktail should be a delight for all the senses. If you cannot get a hold of the proper sticks, use toothpicks instead.

Terminology

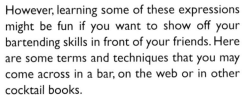

There are some terms and expressions that we have chosen not to use in this book, partly because they may make the recipes incomprehensible (we are aware of the fact that many readers skip the glossary and head straight for the recipes) and partly because we try to stick to everyday language whenever possible.

However, learning some of these expressions might be fun if you want to show off your bartending skills in front of your friends. Here are some terms and techniques that you may come across in a bar, on the web or in other cocktail books.

To **float** means to 'top' the drink with an ingredient – simply to pour some of it on top. You use about 15 ml, or about half an ounce, that you carefully drip in without stirring the drink. Some floats, for example cream floats,

are layered. (Read more about layering on page 18.)

A **splash** is traditionally ¼ of an ounce, or about 7 ml. However, the word is often used to indicate a 'small amount' of liquid, although not quite as small as a 'dash', and frequently when topping a long or short drink with a spray of soda.

A **dash** is about ¹⁄₁₆ of an ounce, or about 2 ml. It is smaller than a 'splash' but is often a subjective measurement. Be careful when talking about a dash of Tabasco or Worcestershire sauce though, in which case 4–5 drops will suffice.

Topping or **filling** is short for 'fill up' and means filling up the drink to the top of the glass with a final liquid, often juice, soda or some other mixer.

Building is the simplest method for making cocktails – simply pour in the spirits one after the other on top of the ice without either stirring too much or shaking.

An **ounce** (oz) is the most common measurement for cocktail liquid ingredients in the United States. In Europe, millilitres is the more common unit. In the UK, shots (about 45 ml or 1 ½ oz) are often used, or simply parts. In this book, we give measurements in both ounces and millilitres to ensure understanding.

S&S stands for 'sweet and sour' and is a time-saving cocktail mix used in many bars. Read more on page 15.

Your Home Bar – Ingredients

Start up your own bar with ingredients according to your own taste. You can achieve a lot with vodka, orange juice and soda. Add your favourite liqueur, and you are off to a good start. Why not let your guests bring a liqueur each and perhaps a mixer while you provide the base spirits (se below), garnishes and ice? It can result in new, exciting flavours and innovative ideas for drinks, perhaps even your own collection of cocktail recipes.

Ingredients that start with a capital letter are registered trademarks from one specific manufacturer. All others are generic names for beverages that may exist in several varieties or under different brand names. For example, the liqueur Cointreau is a trademark and therefore begins with a capital letter, whereas champagne, for example, begins with a lower case letter (as opposed to the Champagne region in France, where the different sorts of champagne are produced).

Before we move on to the liquid ingredients, we need to mention one ingredient that is more important than any other, and which you will (hopefully) not drink – the ice. Good cocktails cannot be made without ice. Why is that, and how does it work?

Ice cubes and **crushed** ice are used to chill drinks, both before and during mixing. Cocktails should be ice cold to ensure that the flavours blossom. You can either chill the ingredients in the refrigerator (or freezer if you are in a rush) or you can stir or shake them together with ice. Crushed ice chills faster than ice cubes, but it also melts faster.

Believe it or not, the quality of the ice can be good or less good. Use newly frozen ice. Old ice melts faster and may dilute the drink. It may also have absorbed unwanted flavours from other foods in the freezer.

Be generous with the ice. A common misconception is that the more ice that is put in your glass, the more diluted your drink becomes, but, in fact, the opposite is true! Ice cubes keep each other cool. A drink with only a couple of ice cubes bobbing on the surface is much more likely to become diluted than a drink in an ice-filled glass. Another false belief is that stingy bartenders fill up the glass with ice to save spirits. 2 oz is always 2 oz, regardless of the amount of ice.

Always make sure to use an ice scoop or ice tongs when filling your glass or shaker with ice. If you use the glass itself, it may break and you have to discard all the ice in the container. Choose a scoop that is slightly smaller than the glass to keep the ice from spilling out on either side of the glass.

A shaker should be at least half-filled with ice, and after shaking, discard the ice. The same goes for stirred drinks. Do not attempt to reuse the ice – firstly because it absorbs flavours from the ingredients and secondly because it will have become wet and thus risks to dilute the drinks. If you plan to serve the drink you have just shaken with ice, scoop up some fresh, steaming cold ice. The glass should be filled almost all the way up.

Cocktails whose ingredients have been mixed with ice in a blender often get the epithet 'frozen' and have a texture that is similar to sorbet. A short drink with ice, served in a short glass with no stem, is called 'on the rocks'. Short drinks in cocktail glasses are served without ice cubes, which makes it even more important to chill them properly in a shaker or a mixing glass before serving.

Base spirits is what we call spirits that are not infused or flavoured in any way. If it says 'base spirits' in one of our recipes, it means that you have a choice between whisky, gin, rum, tequila, brandy and vodka. Below is a brief introduction to these spirits. For more detailed information, see pages 27–33.

Whisky is the godfather of all spirits. It has a faithful army of followers who constantly argue about what kind of whisky is the best. Whisky is produced in many parts of the world today. You will for example be able to find whisky from Japan – sounds interesting, right? The most famous varieties, however, have their origins in the US, Canada, Ireland and Scotland. Ireland and Scotland have a long-standing argument over who was first; some sources claim that whisky was first produced in Scotland as early as in the 15th century.

Many people like the Scottish version, Scotch, for which peat is used in the manufacturing process. It gives it a harsh and smoky flavour, which is different from Irish whisky. In Scotland, all whisky was originally made from malt by means of a method similar to the way beer is brewed. Malt is made from barley. Nowadays, the most common Scottish whiskies are mixtures of grain and malt whiskies. These are simply referred to as 'blended'. And very successful they are too! However, pure malt whisky is still considered the finest. The smoky notes of a single malt

are perhaps not quite right for cocktails but might be better suited solo, on the rocks.

Irish whiskies are milder and fruitier than Scotch, which is partly due to different distilling methods. They are similar in many other ways too, except for the spelling. In Ireland and the US, it is spelt 'whiskey', with an 'e', for some obscure reason. In Canada, both spellings can be found. The American manufacturing process is the most common – without malt and with rye whisky and wheat whisky blended with corn. Canadian whisky and bourbon are often the most suitable options for cocktails. But an Irish Coffee, the world's most famous coffee drink, would of course not be complete without Irish whiskey!

The US is most famous for its bourbon, which is corn-based. Contrary to other whiskies, bourbon is matured in brand new, lightly charred oak casks, from which it develops its vanilla notes. Not surprisingly, it was Irish and Scottish immigrants who first brought whisky to America and began producing it there. Tasty cocktails made with bourbon include Mint Julep, Old Fashioned and Manhattan.

So, how was it again – should it be spelt with or without the 'e'? Oh well, let us agree on a generic spelling without the 'e' to make it simple!

Gin is the favourite of the English . It is made from grain and potatoes, which is something it has in common with other spirits. The difference is, however, that gin is flavoured with juniper berries. London Dry Gin works very well in cocktails as it is distinct but not too sweet in flavour. Many gin cocktails were composed during the Prohibition era in the US, when moonshine became popular and bartenders had to abandon whisky. The reason for this was that whisky would take too long to mature for anyone making it in their bathtub at home. Classic gin cocktails include Dry Martini, Love in an Elevator, Bronx, Gimlet and the illustrious Pink Lady and White Lady.

Rum is made from cane sugar and has its origin in the Caribbean. However, the most famous type is probably Cuban rum, and the national cocktails Mojito and Daiquiri are essential for any who wishes to experience rum culture. There is a multitude of famous rum cocktails: Mai Tai, Piña Colada, Cuba Libre … Cachaça is a slightly sweet Brazilian rum. If you want to try it, make yourself a Caipirinha.

Tequila is the proud national spirit of Mexico. It is made from the agave plant. In cocktails, the clear silver tequila is used unless otherwise stated. The colour of other type, golden tequila, comes from aging. The distinct flavour of tequila goes well with tangy juices. Tequila is mostly used in Margaritas, but also in cocktails such as the romantic Silk Stockings and the rudely named shooter Adios Motherfucker.

Brandy comes in many forms and is often called cognac internationally, but to deserve that name it needs to have been produced in the French province of Cognac. Hard to follow? All types of brandy are made from grapes, which means that they are produced by distilling wine. If you are a great wine-lover, brandy might be the cocktail base for you. Why not try an Alexander, a Sidecar or a Horse's Neck?

Vodka is the most anonymous of all cocktail bases. It barely has any flavour at all unless you count the burning sensation in your throat. There are no signifying flavours or aromas. Might that be one of its strengths, to work in the dark? It lets others shine instead. Cocktails that take advantage of this are, for example, Bloody Mary, Screwdriver, Cosmopolitan and Chocolate Martini. Vodka can be made from potatoes, grain or vegetables (sounds healthy, right?) and is a popular export product mainly of Russia, Poland and Scandinavia. Nowadays, there are plenty of flavoured and infused vodkas in so many different aromas that the only thing that separates vodka from liqueur is that it is not sweet. In a Vanilla Sky, it is the vodka, not the liqueur, that contributes the vanilla note, and in an Absolut Raspberri, it gives the raspberry liqueur a push in the right direction. A little flavouring makes everything possible. However, the day when we can buy whiskey-flavoured vodka, the vodka manufacturers will probably have to deal with a bunch of angry Irishmen …

Liqueurs are highly sweetened flavoured spirits that exist in an infinite number of flavours and colours. They are very popular as a cocktail ingredient. As a substitute, you can use flavoured syrups that come in hundreds of varieties. They consist of fruit juice mixed with sugar. Read more about liqueurs on page 34.

Bitters are highly concentrated and are used in small amounts to add flavour to a cocktail. Most bitters are made from the bark of the Gentian root, whose taste is so bitter that it would be possible to dilute it a million times without it losing its bitterness. Other common ingredients include wormwood and citrus fruits. Bitters were once used as medicine and were thought to aid digestion. You can still buy some bitters in the form of 'digestifs', for example Fernet Branca, Jägermeister and Angostura Bitters. A bitter may be just as sweet as a liqueur or a soft drink, but this may pass unnoticed as the bitter flavours are so dominant. Without the sweetness, they would be undrinkable. In cocktails you often find bitters such as Cinzano Bitter, Rosita, Peychaud's and Regan's orange bitters. Tonic water is the soda version – a soft drink rarely appreciated by youngsters. Angostura Bitters is a well-known brand used for making cocktails. It is rum-based and produced in Trinidad. It is relatively mild and includes flavours such as cardamom, cinnamon and Seville oranges. Mild or not – 5 drops in a glass is enough!

Beer is a fairly unusual ingredient in mixed drinks, but lager is essential when mixing a Shandy. Some types of beer go well with liqueurs, spirits and other mixers. Ginger beer is not really beer, but a tasty, ginger-flavoured soft drink, which is more intense than ginger ale. It is for example used for making Moscow Mules.

White wine. Be sure to choose a dry white for mixed drinks, unless the recipe states differently.

Red wine used in mixed drinks should be light or medium-bodied.

Champagne is what we call the sparkling white wine that is produced exclusively in the French region of Champagne according to the Méthode Champenoise. Champagne is a legally protected term, and no matter how delicious and professionally produced the wine is, it may not be called champagne unless it has been produced in the Champagne region. For so-called champagne cocktails, a medium-priced sparkling wine, a dry Spanish cava for example, is sufficient. For a classic Bellini, the Italian Prosecco of the original recipe, is the best choice.

Port wine is a fortified wine produced in the Douro Valley in Portugal.

Sherry is another fortified wine, but it has Spanish origins. In cocktails, use a dry sherry.

Dubonnet is a sweet and flavoursome fortified wine with bitter notes, which is produced in France.

Vermouth is a wine fortified with strong spirit and herbs – wormwood for example. It is a very popular cocktail ingredient. Red vermouth has a rather sweet taste while white vermouth comes in both sweet and dry versions. Classic drinks with vermouth include Dry Martini, Bronx and Rob Roy. Vermouth is also a delicious treat to enjoy on its own. Martini is probably the most well-known brand of vermouth, not to be confused with the cocktail Martini. Other famous brands are Noilly Prat and Lillet.

NON-ALCOHOLIC INGREDIENTS

Juices that are popular mixers include cranberry juice, orange juice, pineapple juice and grapefruit juice. Short drinks with a higher concentration of alcohol and not containing a mixer often include lime or lemon juice instead.

You can find bottled lime and lemon juice in the shops, but the best result always comes from pressing them yourself. A medium-sized lemon contains about 1 ½ oz or 45 ml of juice and a lime about 1 oz (30 ml). An orange normally contains about 2 oz (60 ml).

Simple syrup is a very common ingredient in the recipes in this book. It is easy to prepare at home. Simply bring equal parts sugar and water to a boil in a saucepan on the stove. Simple syrup is usually made with white sugar, but for tropical drinks, try cane sugar or Demerara sugar for a richer flavour. When the granules have dissolved, the syrup is ready. Another option is to prepare the syrup directly in the bottle instead of in the saucepan, provided that the bottle is heat-proof. Shake the sugar with hot water from the kettle. You can store the syrup in a bottle in the refrigerator for about two weeks. It is also possible to buy ready-made bottled sugar syrup in food shops.

Rose's Lime Cordial is a sweetened lime juice that is suitable if the ingredients include 'sour mix'. Make your own lime cordial by mixing equal parts freshly squeezed lime juice and simple syrup, or a little sugar. If you want a less sour cocktail, replace the lime juice with lime cordial.

Syrup is a sugary liquid made from fruits, berries, nuts or herbs in highly concentrated form. Syrups are used as a condiment in cocktails as an alternative to sugar or fresh fruit – or as a substitute for liqueur in non-alcoholic cocktails. Grenadine is an example of a highly popular pomegranate-flavoured syrup in the world of cocktail-making (see below).

Sugar is the basic ingredient of simple syrup, but it can also be used in solid form when making cocktails. It is very important, however, that the sugar granules dissolve completely so that they do not crunch between your teeth when enjoying the cocktail. Sugar does not dissolve completely in alcohol, which means that you have to dissolve it in a mixer first, juice, for example. The most suitable type of sugar is normally indicated in the recipe. If the recipe simply says 'sugar', superfine caster sugar is a good choice. In older cocktail books, icing sugar is sometimes indented. Some cocktails, for example many Margaritas, have a frosted rim of sugar (read more about this term below).

Raw sugar is unrefined cane or beet sugar. It is brown in colour with a spicy flavour on top of the sweetness. It is a good choice for tropical drinks.

White sugar is refined (purified) to get rid of the husks, which means it loses its colour and nutrients. What is left is a pure, white product with a neutral, sweet taste.

Icing sugar is white sugar that has been ground into a powder.

Muscovado sugar, produced in Mauritius, is very popular in the UK. It is very lightly refined in order to retain its colour and flavour. It has a spicier flavour than brown sugar. There are two types of Muscovado sugar: one is dark with a hint of liquorice and the other light with a caramel note. It works well in desserts, especially chocolate desserts.

Rock sugar, sometimes called rock candy, is golden crystals of cane sugar. It was a popular treat for children in the olden days. Today, it is used by Belgian beer manufacturers to aid yeast fermentation (ales, abbey and Trappist beers). Rock sugar does not add any flavour during the process, but it makes the beer stronger than normal beer (6–8 %). Rock sugar contributes a taste of caramel to tropical cocktails.

Brown sugar is a mixture of refined sugar crystals and dark brown cane sugar syrup (the basis of normal white sugar). It has a more neutral flavour than Muscovado sugar and is therefore often used in cooking. It is, for example, very popular in Irish Coffee.

Sour mix is a ready-made substitute for simple syrup and lemon juice that is used in many bars. The mix can be bought as a powder to which you add water. If you often make drinks with sour mix, such as Margaritas, you can make your own by mixing 3/5 lemon juice and 2/5 simple syrup (read more under 'simple syrup'). It can be stored for about two weeks in the refrigerator. Lime cordial, e.g. Rose's lime, is a kind of liquid sour mix sold by the bottle.

Grenadine is mainly used because of its strong red colour. It is responsible for the sunrise in a Tequila Sunrise, and the pink guise of a Pink Lady. The flavour is intensely sweet. For this reason it is used in very small amounts. Grenadine was originally made from pomegranate juice, but today a factory-made syrup that contains a mix of several different red berries and sugar is more commonly used.

Mixers are non-alcoholic liquids used for filling up long drinks. Besides different sorts of juice, a variety of carbonated drinks will make your home bar complete. Stock up on lemonade, club soda, tonic water, ginger ale and cola.

Coffee is loved all over the world, and it is of course used in many different kinds of cocktails (anything from elegant French Coffee to exotic Jamaican Coffee). Hot drinks with coffee are not served in cups, but in heat-proof cocktail glasses with a handle or a stem to hold.

Egg white is used in some cocktails when you want a bit of froth in your glass after shaking, which is sometimes the case with sours and fizzes. You can buy ready-made cocktail froth if you do not want to use raw egg due to the risk of salmonella.

Coconut milk is the milk found in fresh coconuts. It is a common ingredient in tropical drinks such as Piña Colada. There is also the sweet and sticky cream of coconut, but if you are looking for a thickener, we recommend using coconut cream instead, which is simply a more concentrated form of coconut milk.

Lemon or **orange twist** is a method whereby the peel of a citrus fruit is twisted until a drop of citrus oil is released. The peel should be 2–3 cm long (about 1 inch) and is twisted

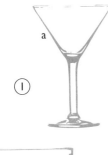

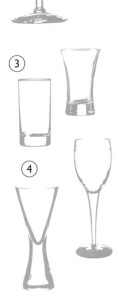

over the glass. The oil adds extra spice to the drink, and the peel looks nice as a garnish if you drop it into the glass afterwards. Try to use organic, washed fruit whenever possible.

Herbs and **spices**. Mint, nutmeg, cinnamon, black pepper, coarse sea salt, ginger, chilli, coriander … everything is allowed in cocktail-making nowadays. The list of flavours is endless.

Glassware

Why use different glasses for different cocktails – would not a normal glass do? It might, as a matter of fact. But then the cocktail experience would not be complete, which would be a shame considering the effort invested in the preparation and, hopefully, the freshness of the ingredients.

The choice of glass can be simple – a glass with a stem to hold prevents the hand from warming up a cocktail without ice, thus ruining the experience. But the choice of glass can also be as complex as its content. Different glasses bring out different qualities of the concoction. There are of course more glass types than we have listed here. Below you can read about the most common ones.

Cocktails can be divided into two groups – long drinks and short drinks. Short drinks, like pre-dinner aperitifs, are, as the name implies, intended for swift drinking. As they consist of strong spirits only, they are served in a short, more elegant glass. In long drinks, however, the cocktail base is diluted with a large quantity of mixers – juice, soda or tonic – in order to make the drink last longer and quench the thirst. Filling up a highball with alcohol only would probably not be such a good idea …

SHORT DRINKS

A **cocktail glass** (1), sometimes called Martini glass, is a conical glass on a tall stem. There are two types: the normal and the 'double', for the extra thirsty. In this glass, cool classics

such as Dry Martini, Manhattan or Sidecar are served. The *Martini glass* (1a) automatically gives the holder an elegant, sophisticated look, regardless of outfit. The *Margarita glass* (1b) is another kind of cocktail glass that looks a bit like an upside-down sombrero. Both glasses look lovely with a frosted rim (read more about this below).

A **champagne glass** (2) is used for well-known champagne cocktails such as Ritz Fizz and Bellini. They come in two different versions:

Flutes (2a) are tall and narrow, and *coupes* (2b) are classy, wide-mouthed glasses on an elegant stem. Flutes preserve the bubbles better, but many think that the coupe looks more glamorous, perhaps because it evokes images of beautiful champagne pyramids with champagne flowing from the top layer and onto the next in a fantastic fountain. The choice of glass is a matter of taste, but if you like bubbles, go for the flute.

A champagne tasting glass has a lower, more rounded bowl which helps bring out the bouquet of an aged, less carbonated, champagne. A coupe is a good choice for a real, aged champagne or a more exclusive sparkling wine that have a lot more to offer than bubbles. The designer of the coupe is said to have been inspired by the royal breasts of Queen Marie Antoinette – now that is luxury!

A **shot glass** (3) is the smallest glass type. It is used for shots and shooters – and, if desired, as a measuring glass.

A **liqueur glass** (4) sometimes looks like a miniature wine glass and is intended for liqueurs – strong alcoholic beverages which, unlike shots, are meant for sipping and are generally drunk on their own, without mixers.

A **rocks glass**, a **whisky glass** and an **old-fashioned glass** (5) are more or less the same, but there are small variations. They are short, with straight edges and no stem. (A whisky tasting glass, on the other hand, has a small bowl on a stem.)

A *rocks glass* is slightly taller than the others, with a wider mouth, and as the name suggests, it is often used for drinks that are served 'on the rocks' – over ice.

Old Fashioned is a drink that has given its name to a glass. The old-fashioned glass looks like a whisky glass, but it has a sturdier, concave base, which makes it suitable for muddling. This glass is sometimes simply called a tumbler. It holds more liquid than a cocktail glass, as it has to fit the obligatory ice. It is hardly necessary to include all three glasses in your collection, one is enough. Pick your favourite.

To make matters simple, we refer to short glasses without a stem (except for shot glasses) simply as **tumblers** in the recipes.

A **snifter** (6), or brandy glass, has a short stem and a large, round bowl, perfect for cupping your hands around in order to warm up the contents slightly. The narrowing neck further helps to capture and concentrate the unique personality of a brandy and brings the aroma to your nostrils in an exceptionally enjoyable manner. Take a deep breath, inhale the lovely aroma and prepare your taste buds before taking a sip – this is part of the experience. But watch out! Do not put your nose as far down the glass as you might do at a wine tasting – it will make the experience too intense and bring tears to your eyes while your taste buds will only experience a 'heavy alcohol odour'. Hold your glass at waist-level instead, and you will experience the fantastic bouquet of a fine brandy (but do not use it in a cocktail, a plainer brandy will do for that purpose). The snifter is rarely used for cocktails, but sometimes for serving a liqueur 'on the rocks'.

LONG DRINKS
A **highball glass** (7) is the most common glass for long drinks. It is tall and narrow and holds about 6–10 oz (180–300 ml) of liquid, which is a normal amount for these types of cocktails. It has plenty of room for ice, and you often fill it up to the brim with ice cubes.

A **Collins glass** (8) is often taller and has a wider mouth than a highball. Sometimes, tall highball glasses are referred to as Collins glasses. They can hold about 12–17 oz (350–500 ml) and are appropriate for Long Island Iced Teas and other large volume cocktails.

A **Hurricane glass** (9) is spacious and has an exotic shape that brings the Caribbean and other sunny places to mind. With the right beach drink inside, it will make any summer sizzle!

This glass was named for its shape, which is similar to that of a hurricane lamp. Some well-known drinks usually served in this glass are Piña Colada and Tequila Sunrise. The glass carries a parasol well, and also heavy garnishes like chunks of pineapple and coconut.

Large wine glasses (10) can hold large amounts and are suitable for cocktails based on wine or ice-cream. They are sometimes used for hot drinks since you can hold the stem instead of the bowl. However, an Irish Coffee mug is even more appropriate for this purpose.

An **Irish Coffee mug** (11) has a short stem and a handle that allows you to hold the glass without burning your hands – and it is, of course, heatproof. If you prefer using a wine glass for your hot drinks, prepare the glass by rinsing it in hot water first. Leave a metal spoon in the glass while pouring the hot drink – the spoon conducts the heat and prevents it from cracking. To be on the safe side, do not choose your finest crystal wine glasses.

Techniques

Chilling the glass is necessary for drinks that are served without ice, normally short drinks in Martini or Margarita glasses. You can chill a glass using either of these two methods: put the glass in the freezer for 5 minutes – or 10 minutes if you want a frosted glass. Alternatively, fill up the glass with ice, leave it for a while, then discard the ice.

⑥

⑦

⑧

⑨

⑩

⑪

A **salt** or **sugar rim** is made by decoratively coating the rim of a glass with salt or sugar, most commonly a Martini or Margarita glass. A salt rim is traditionally found with the classic Margarita, where the salt is part of the taste experience. A sugared rim is more of a decoration and can be part of almost any cocktail, but goes especially well with fruity Margaritas.

The best choice for the salt rim of a Margarita is coarse sea salt. If you want a fun colour effect for your sugar rim, dip the glass into a saucer with food colouring or Curaçao instead of moistening it with a lime or lemon wedge. You can make a rim with almost anything: grated chocolate, cinnamon, finely chopped nuts, sprinkles or black pepper.

Instructions: Pour salt (or whatever else you have chosen) onto a saucer. Carefully cut into a lime or lemon wedge and run it over the rim of the glass – hold the glass upside-down so as to avoid spilling juice on it. Then, dip the rim into the salt, and the salt crystals will set nicely around the rim. You can also try rolling the glass – choose the technique that you prefer. The goal is an even, nice rim and a dry glass.

Layering is the method to use when you want the liquids to form layers on top of each other without mixing. This can create wonderful stripy colour effects, for example in shooters, or allow the cream in hot drinks to lie as an elegant blanket of snow on top of the rich, dark brown drink. To succeed with layering, you need to know which of the different liquids has the highest density, in other words, which of them is the heaviest. Sugar is heavy, and sweet spirits with low alcohol content weigh more than unsweetened, highly alcoholic spirits. Luckily, you do not always have to keep track of this yourself – in most recipes it is clear in which order the ingredients should be added. The pouring technique, however, demands some skill and practice.

Instructions: Pour the ingredient that is mentioned first into the glass. Then, pour the next ingredient slowly and over the back of a spoon that is held close to the edge of the glass. Repeat the procedure with the next liquid, and so on.

Layered drinks had their heyday in the late 19th and the early 20th century. In Europe, bartenders would call these drinks *pousse-cafés*, spectacular creations where layer upon layer of spirits and liqueurs would create eye-catching effects. They were served in elegant, tall glasses on a short stem, which are to this day called *pousse-café glasses* – and you can fit many layers in one of those!

SHAKE, STIR OR BLEND?
Why do we shake some cocktails?

We shake to mix as well as to chill. Some ingredients refuse to mix with others. A few good shakes are required as persuasion. Reluctant ingredients include juices, cream, viscous liqueurs, simple syrup and egg white. You need a bit of force to make them cooperate. But there are, of course, cocktails that are based on the stirring technique, and sometimes not even that. This may partly be due to the flavour effect that is achieved when the ingredients are separated from one another in the glass, or perhaps simply float on the surface, and partly for the purpose of colour: what would a Tequila Sunrise be without its dawn?

Cocktails in tall-stemmed glasses are often served without ice. That is why it is necessary to shake them with plenty of ice in a shaker – alternatively, stir them with ice – to ensure that the ingredients are properly chilled. A cocktail served without ice is often served in a cocktail glass with a stem you can hold to prevent your hand from warming the contents. That is the reason why the glass has a stem (not to provide a sophisticated look – that comes as a bonus).

Since most **short drinks** are served in tumblers over ice cubes – 'on the rocks' – or with crushed ice, shaking or stirring them for chilling purposes is not always necessary. However, if the spirits come straight from the bar at room temperature, it will have negative consequences on the ice in the glass, which will immediately start to melt. Shaking is of course fun, but if you do not feel like doing it, put your bottles in the refrigerator instead (or, if you are in a hurry, in the freezer).

Long drinks are normally not shaken for chilling purposes. When you fill them up with a large amount of chilled juice or soda, the drink will be sufficiently chilled anyway. Besides, it will most likely be served with ice cubes in the glass. When shaking is involved, it is often because the ingredients need to be properly mixed. When you want the final creation to have a bit of froth, shaking usually achieves this too. But beware! Never shake carbonated liquids! If you want to give it a try – do your cocktail-making in the bathtub.

Frozen cocktails are blended with ice to a smooth, ice-cream-like consistency. If you want to use whole chunks of fruit, use a kitchen blender. You can also replace fresh fruit with ready-made fruit purees.

MEASURING

When you start to mix cocktails, you will soon notice that the proportions for a drink may vary considerably between different recipes, and sometimes even different ingredients are given. That is actually no stranger than the fact that Bolognese recipes vary from one cookbook to another – some chefs prefer grated carrots in their sauce, some not. No recipe is set in stone.

The same applies to cocktails. Mix according to your own personal taste, which may result in your very own version of one of the old classics. But more often than not, there is a standard recipe, and we have aimed to include this as well as fun variations in this book. Experimenting with new, innovative versions is not something you have to put off until after a bartending course.

Perhaps your imagination will start to flow after a night of cocktail mixing in the company of friends, or a new cocktail will see the light of day simply because you forgot to buy one of the ingredients required. The apple liqueur in an Appletini could one day be swapped for apple juice, which might be replaced by your favourite grapefruit breakfast juice the next, which may in turn be exchanged for some Cointreau left over from Christmas. To lose a bit of respect can be a good thing. There is only one rule – if it tastes good, drink it! Everything is up to you. Then there are the immortal classics: Dry Martini, Mojito, Manhattan and Gin Tonic, for example. It would be a sin not to at least try the original version first. There is a reason why it has become immortal.

The total amount of spirits in a cocktail determines its strength. In Europe, the amount of spirits is often given in millilitres, with 40 or 60 millilitres as the standard measurement. In Anglophone countries, matters are a little more complicated. The Imperial fluid ounce equals 28.4 ml, and the American 29.6 ml, which is quite close. The most important thing, however, is to keep the same balance between the different ingredients. When you are making the drink weaker or stronger, remember to adjust the other ingredients too. Some drinks traditionally contain a large amount of alcohol as they include several different types of spirits and liqueurs. A Long Island Iced Tea, for example, often contains about 3 ½ oz of spirits (100 ml), although hopefully it lasts a little longer...

GARNISHES, DECORATION AND PRESENTATION

Much of the glamour surrounding cocktails lies in the garnishes. Feel free to use your imagination. There are no fixed rules, even though some cocktails are forever associated with a certain 'guise': an olive in the Dry Martini feels almost like a necessity, for example. A feminine, red maraschino cherry is of course very striking in a Manhattan and will almost certainly match the lipstick of somebody who wants to make an unforgettable impression. In exotic drinks such as Piña Colada, you expect a parasol and probably some heavy fruit chunks hanging off the rim of the glass – pineapple or coconut perhaps.

Then there are cocktails for which it is unclear whether the garnish is intended as a flavour enhancer or decoration. Maybe both, as in the case of the mint in a Mojito, or the limes in a Caipirinha.

Sometimes the garnish itself gives rise to a new cocktail, or at any rate a new version of one. A bartender was once asked to make a Dry Martini, but had run out of olives. He thought for a moment, and then dropped a pickled onion into the glass instead. The Gibson cocktail was born.

Garnishes can also hang off the rim of the glass, float on the surface or be put on a skewer together with other fruits, berries or even vegetables.

The choice of garnish depends on the cocktail you have in mind. Most commonly, bartenders use an ingredient that is already part of the drink, but this is in no way a strict rule. Berries and fruits are fun to use as decoration, but beware of the cocktail turning into a fruit salad. The old adage 'less is more' applies here too. A single rose petal floating on the surface of a Martini glass can give the cocktail an almost magical appearance.

Do not forget to bring home lots of fruit. The morning after, you can always make a refreshing detox smoothie with the leftovers …

Here are some ideas for garnishes:

- olives, black and green

- maraschino cherries, red and green

- lime, orange and lemon peel, twirls, twists, wedges, wheels and slices

- blueberries, raspberries, strawberries, cherries, grapes and other berries on a skewer – and remember that the leaves are often just as decorative!

- exotic fruits such as kiwi, pineapple, carambola and cumquat

- sliced apples and peaches

- sliced bananas

- celery sticks (for tomato based cocktails such as Bloody Mary)

- grated chocolate

- coffee beans and powder

- nutmeg

- cardamom

- cinnamon

- whole spices such as cloves, cinnamon sticks, bay leaves and peppercorns

- fresh herbs, leaves from fruits and berries

- flowers (edible ones, of course) such as rose and elderflower

- corny decorations like pea pods or fir twigs? Using your imagination and choosing something that fits the season is never wrong.

- coloured ice or frozen berries

- coloured salt or sugar rim

A bartender once ran out of red maraschino cherries and used green ones instead.
Customer: 'What's that green stuff in my Manhattan?'
Bartender: 'But sir, don't you see that it's Central Park?'

By Örjan Westerlund

Distilling Spirits

THE BASICS OF DISTILLATION

The first step in the manufacture of spirits is to find a product with high sugar content. This product is used to produce a fermentable liquid such as wort or grape must, which is fermented until it reaches a certain alcohol content. This turns the liquid into mash or wine which can later be distilled.

Distillation is a way of concentrating the most volatile compound in a mixture made up of several liquids. In this case, it entails increasing the alcohol content of the fermented liquid and losing some of the water. If the liquid is distilled several times, the lighter compound, i.e. the alcohol, reaches a higher, level of concentration with each step. This occurs, for instance, with spirits that are distilled rather primitively, in copper stills. A typical example is Scotch, which is normally distilled twice and thus has a lower alcohol content than Irish whiskey, which is often distilled three times. If distillation is performed on an industrial scale, in so-called column stills, it may be done in several steps and dozens of times in the same still. One example is the 90 distillations it takes to produce the well-known agricultural product Absolut Vodka.

THE RAW MATERIALS

As mentioned above, the raw material has to contain sugar, or starch that can be transformed into fermentable sugar. In other words, ordinary sugar bought at the supermarket will do. It is perhaps the most common ingredient in moonshine. In other cases, the sugar comes from the vegetable kingdom: from cane sugar, barley, corn, agave, grapes, potatoes or different sorts of fruit. Whether or not the ingredients need to be processed in order to access the sugar determines the first step of the distillation process. In several cases – agave, potatoes, barley and cane sugar – the material needs to be processed in order

to break up the starch, i.e. the energy storing constituent of the plant – since starch itself is not fermentable. In order to break down the long carbohydrates into simpler, fermentable sugars, either the natural enzymes (amylases) in, for example, barley are used, or, alternatively, enzymes in combination with high pressure and high temperature. This may be exemplified with potatoes that are pressure-cooked before they are fermented into mash and later distilled. Read more about the materials and the primary steps in the manufacture of spirits under *Cocktail bases* on page 27.

THE TWO MAIN PRINCIPLES OF DISTILLATION

The discovery of the principles of distillation is believed to have occurred when man first noticed that vessels warmed by the sun lose part of their content through evaporation, while others become concentrated. Compare this to what happens if you leave lemonade out in the sun – as the hours go by, it gets sweeter at the same time as it decreases in volume.

This discovery was used by alchemists and others throughout the centuries. Eventually, it made its way to Europe where the distillation of wine for medical purposes became common in the early Middle Ages. The process was discovered in the Middle East, and the production process was not unlike the way we manufacture the raw spirit of what we today call matured spirits, for instance brandy and malt whisky.

BATCH DISTILLATION IN POT STILLS

This ancient distillation method involves heating up the liquid in a vessel that normally looks like a built-over cauldron, and then collect the vapour, which is collected by the stillhead. It then proceeds into the chimney-like *swan's neck*, which guides the vapour into a condenser. The resulting product, that has a higher alcohol content, is called *distillate*. The distillate then runs out of the condenser and into a collection tank. The distillation process is usually repeated once or twice depending on the type of spirit that is being manufactured. The distillate from the first pot usually has such a low alcohol content (around 20–25 per cent) that a second distillation is necessary to achieve the strength typical of strong spirits. In the final distillation run, the alcohol that comes out of the still is divided into three parts as time goes by and the temperature rises.

Initially, the compounds with the lowest boiling point will evaporate and flow out of the pot's condenser in liquid form. This is usually called the *head*. As distillation continues, the temperature rises to a point when the drinkable alcohol, *ethanol*, emerges from the still. The product that is the result of this part of the process is called the *heart*, and is put aside for later maturing. As the temperature continues to rise, the drinkable compounds have completely evaporated and the distillate is no longer desirable. At this point, the distillate mainly consists of heavy substances with high boiling points that still have enough energy to separate themselves from the liquid in the still. This final third of the distillate is called the *tail*. Both the head and the tail are saved as they, in this inexact chemical process, still contain ethanol that can be distilled again together with the next batch of mash.

Finally, we will mention something about the pot still. It is synonymous with alambic, the Arabic word for this type of still. This expression is used mainly in France, but also in other parts of the world.

CONTINUOUS DISTILLATION IN COLUMN STILLS

At the end of the 18th and the beginning of the 19th centuries, especially the British started to experiment with new still models, and connected them in order to improve their effect. The continuous distillation method was patented in 1831. An Irish former tax commissioner, Aeneas Coffey, who lent his name to the still, had by then enhanced an earlier version of the still to such a degree that the modern column still could see the light of day. This invention solved several problems. For instance, it now became possible to produce spirits of much higher purity, and the process could be continuous, a fact that rendered the manufacture much more efficient as there was no need to keep interrupting the process in order to clean the still and reload it with new mash.

The column still has two columns – an analyser and a rectifier. The working principle of the still is that the mash is preheated by being led into a pipe that winds through the rectifier. The pipe then continues to the top of the vapour-heated analyser column. There, the mash drips down onto perforated metal plates. The heat makes the mash evaporate, and the vapour is conducted back into the base of the rectifier column where it gradually rises through the perforated plates. For every step, the ethanol content of the vapour increases, and, eventually, it has been refined into ethanol, which often very strong and thus very pure. Complicated? Sure, but very efficient industrially speaking.

POT STILL SPIRIT VERSUS RECTIFIED SPIRIT?

Just like beauty is in the eye of the beholder, the notion of what is a good quality spirit depends on what you intend to use it for. Depending on whether you are a chemist and want your spirit pure, or whether you want a flavoursome and aromatic after-dinner drink with your coffee, judgments vary. On the one hand, the pot still is cumbersome, inefficient and inexact. On the other hand, it produces a type of spirit that has plenty of character and crude alcohol that is unique for every manufacturer, and also suitable for maturing. One explanation is that these stills, after a double distillation, produce spirits with an alcohol content of only about 70 per cent. Impurities produce reactions over time, both with the maturing cask and the surroundings.

The neutral spirit that is the result of distillation in a column still may, on the other hand, be pure or as good as pure, that is to say around 96 per cent alcohol by volume in strength. Hence, it does not retain much of the original character of the raw material. What is lacking are the light and heavy chemical compounds that characterise the head and tail of a pot still distillation – esters, aldehydes, ketones, terpenes and fusel oils. The presence of impurities is not necessarily a disadvantage, however, it depends on what the product is intended for. Sometimes the spirit is taken out of the still while the alcohol content is low for the very reason that you want it to retain some of the substances that disappear when it reaches a higher purity, since they add flavour. Contrary to myth, when making fine, matured spirits, fusel and other impurities are in fact desirable in the raw materials in limited amounts.

The usage of the different spirit types can be generalised in different ways: for example, neutral spirit is not matured, but watered down until it reaches the appropriate strength for commercial use (about 37–40 per cent), which is the case with, for example, vodka. Pot still spirit, on the other hand, retains the character of the raw material – regardless of whether it was barley, corn, agave, grapes or molasses – and may be fruity and rich or harsh, oily and even unpleasant if not matured. The components that contribute to this are also the reason why column still spirits benefit from maturing. Typical examples of matured spirits of this kind are malt whisky, calvados, brandy and certain types of dark rum.

FROM RAW SPIRIT TO FINAL PRODUCT

Regardless of origin, raw spirit is colourless, or possibly crystal clear with an almost icy, blue hue. The taste and smell of raw spirit can vary enormously; it may be mild, neutral, harsh or rich in flavour. However, due to the distilling process it never contains sugar, even though the taste of the ethanol itself may appear sweet. The way in which these qualities are used or toned down depends on the final product and the producer's objectives.

The raw spirit is always processed before it is bottled for commercial purposes. This is done through a combination of carbon filtering, flavouring, colouring, maturing, and, of course, dilution. The purpose is to make it taste milder or to give it more character, sometimes both. In connection with what we might call flavouring, de facto purely cosmetic measures, the sweetening and colouring of spirits can be mentioned. Vodka, for example, is sweetened to round off the harshness and give it a milder impression; however, the amount of sugar is not greater than a couple of grams per litre. Another example is plain dark rum, which is often sweetened to a greater extent, or liqueurs for which a sugar content of above 100 grams of sugar per litre is normal.

Aging is a highly complex process. There is still uncertainty regarding the details of what actually happens during the process, but the maturing process can be said to both add and remove substances from the spirits. In addition, it contributes to the development of new substances. As an example of the three effects mentioned above, the fact that the light, unwanted substances are the first to evaporate during the aging process. Additionally, lactones, tannins, colour and, as we mentioned earlier, vanillin and sugars are added to the distillate. If the casks have been used previously for other beverages, extra flavour and aromas are added. For example, a former sherry cask adds a taste of raisins, nuts and chocolate. Finally, reactions occur with, for example, alcohol and acids, which unite to form esters that add fruity and spicy flavours. Around 70 per cent of the character of a malt whisky stems from the cask. Consequently, we may concluded that aging is very important for aromatic spirits, even though caramel colouring and wood chips may be the reason for the simpler, and often much harsher, qualities of cheap aromatic spirits.

'If a man wants to impress a woman,
he does it with champagne.
If he wants to impress another man,
he does it with brandy.'
Unknown

Cocktail Bases

By Örjan Westerlund

Vodka

According to current EU legislation, vodka can be manufactured from all sorts of agricultural products, which means that wheat as well as potatoes and grapes may be used. However, wood is no longer allowed within the European Union, since it is not considered an agricultural product.

Vodka, a Russian diminutive for water, was originally a cereal product brought to Northern Europe by soldiers campaigning in the east. In the Western world today, vodka is mainly used as a cocktail base. In the countries around the Baltic Sea, it is also used as a base for herb-flavoured aquavit. In terms of volume sold, the production is almost exclusively based on distillates from columns stills. An alcohol content of 96 per cent is required for the raw, or basic, spirit used.

It may be flavoured with a small amount of sugar, or with spirits flavoured by the leaching of barley or rye. Another way of flavouring vodka is by adding matured spirits from pot stills. The purpose is to round off the flavour and bring out the character of the raw material.

The manufacture of herb spirits such as aquavit may be done through the process of 'maceration', which means soaking the herbs in the alcohol. Herb spirits sold today are often a mixture of plain spirits and different macerates, which have been re-distilled to remove colour and concentrate aromas.

The largest market for vodka today is the United States. There, pricing in combination with marketing has led to a classification that divides vodka into, for example, 'premium' and 'super premium' qualities. However, the price does not necessarily reflect production costs or quality of the product.

When it comes to flavour, the character of vodka can be varied by the addition of sweeteners and flavourings that add sweetness, crop elements, fruitiness, citrus tones or a pure alcohol flavour.

Tequila and Mezcal

This Mexican distillate is probably connected with more myths and untruths than any other type of spirits. The only way in which an alcoholic beverage may be called tequila is if it has been manufactured in the Jalisco region or one of a few other Mexican districts. It is made from the blue agave, a succulent plant related to the yucca palm, and by no means a cactus, which is often claimed. After harvesting the agave, the leaves are removed with a knife and the remaining heart, the *piña*, which can weigh up to 100 kg, is cut up after which it undergoes a heating process to break down the starch. The juice, *pulque*, is then extracted, fermented and later distilled.

Forty-nine per cent of the ingredients in Tequila may derive from other sources than the agave. In its blended state it is called *mixto*, which can be compared to, for example, a blended whisky. Tequila is sold in several different age categories of which the clear spirit – *plata*, white or silver – is the most common. The yellowish tequila is called *golden*. The finest varieties get their colour from the aging process; simpler types are often coloured with caramel. For a tequila that has been aged properly in wooden tanks or casks, look for the word *reposado* on the label. However, a real connoisseur keeps going through the shelves until he or she finds a bottle with the epithet *añejo*. This means that the tequila has been aged longer and in smaller barrels, and has thus developed more oak character and roundness.

Mexican spirits made from other types of agave than the blue are called mezcal. These have been made notorious by the larva that is sometimes found in the bottle. The original purpose of this worm was to prove that the alcohol content was high enough to preserve the worm intact. Mezcal often has a distinctly smoky taste as the piñas are roasted in ovens fired by charcoal.

The character of un-aged tequila is often very dry, peppery, vegetal and grassy with notes reminiscent of green pepper. As is the case with other aged spirits, the character of the original vegetal matter decreases with age, leaving room for a stronger barrel character. This means less of the fresh, green tone and a greater influence from the previously used American bourbon casks.

Gin

Gin is made with column still spirits as the most common base. Historically speaking, gin is related to the sweeter and oilier Dutch genever. Gin was originally a much sweeter product than the London Dry Gin that dominates the market today. The word 'gin' is an anglicised version of genever, which in turn originates from the Latin word for juniper, *juniperus*, whose berries give the spirit its flavour. Common herbs besides juniper berries include coriander, angelica root and citrus peel. Plain gin is produced by adding essence. The larger brands use more traditional production methods, which usually means maceration of the herbs (see vodka above) followed by a second distillation. In some cases, flavour can also be added by hanging a basket of herbs inside the neck of the column still. The steam absorbs the flavour on its way out. It is somewhat similar to infusing a teabag in a cup of hot water.

Herb Spirits

Other herb spirits than gin and aquavit are produced from column distillate, or in more expensive cases, pot distillate. One example is the classic aperitif and refresher pastis. It is flavoured mainly with aniseed or star anise, and often has a distinct flavour of wormwood. Absinthe has a similar flavouring, but the wormwood is more prominent. Pastis has a high alcohol content and is as a rule mixed with a little water and ice, which makes it cloudy – it 'opalises'.

Among herbs spirits, we might also mention bitter spirits, even though these are perhaps more suitable for post-dinner intake. The term derives from the somewhat harsh flavour of wormwood. Other herbs commonly used in bitters include liquorice, citrus peel and many more, as well a large amount of sugar.

Rum

When the vegetable matter that provides the fermentable sugar is sugar cane, the end product may be called rum. There are two schools regarding the first steps of the production of this spirit. There is the lavish, refined French method, by which sugar cane juice is first made and then used as a basis for distillation. This is less common than the other school, the less costly British version whereby sugar is first made from sugar cane. The by-product of this process, the molasses, then provides the basis for distillation. 'The British way' also means an extra penny in the pocket since the sugar will already have been sold once. Rum is distilled in pot stills as well as column stills. Blending is common. The column stills are often very old and may be even made out of wood. Maturing takes place in oak barrels that may have been used one time too many, which results in a stale, woody taste. When new barrels are used, they replace often used bourbon casks.

Rum is divided into three main categories depending on colour, which is the result of the aging process: *white, gold* and *dark* rum. However, drawing direct parallels between colour and aging is difficult, as some white rum has been aged but deprived of colour through carbon filtering. Similarly, dark rum can get its colour from caramel rather than aging and maturity.

THE RUM PALETTE: WHITE, GOLD AND DARK

White rum is today one of the world's best selling spirits. It is fruity, pure and more or less sharp depending on the amount of sugar added, and, as mentioned above, whether or not it has been aged. Aged white rum is not unusual, but the colour is then removed by filtering. The most common production method is column distillation with molasses as a base, which produces a pure spirit with a neutral, fruity character. There are some examples of grassier, richer types where sugar cane juice has been used as distillation base.

Rum with 'gold' on the label has, unsurprisingly, a golden colour and a slightly sweeter tone than white rum. Gold types are therefore somewhere in between when it comes to flavour, and share some traits with fine dark rum, albeit to a lesser extent. Typical notes can be those of ripe fruit, banana, arrack, fudge and additionally faintly chemical hints of ethyl acetate – something like glue or nail polish remover. Within this intermediate class of rums, we may also encounter spiced sorts where flavours such as vanilla have been added.

Dark rum is generally a good buy considering its age and the fact that the aging process is significantly shorter in the Caribbean than in, for example, a cold warehouse on the Scottish Atlantic coast. Despite this, however, it is well worth noting that the aromas and flavours of a rum that is 8 or 15 years of age may on the one hand be incredible, but on the other rather flat and harsh from caramelized sugar and, in the worst case, old barrels that have seen better days. At its best, dark rum can offer you cascades of smooth and rich flavours such as ripe bananas, vanilla, plum pudding, sultanas, Muscovado sugar, liquorice, caramel, fudge and nuts. A fine dark rum is hard to beat as an after-dinner drink, and thrives in the company of a dark and sweet Maduro cigar.

Brandy, Cognac, Armagnac and Other Fruit Spirits

Brandy is perhaps the best-known and most traditional of all after-dinner drinks. More specifically, brandy from the region of Cognac, north of Bordeaux, France. Brandy is generally a distillate of wine, in some cases connected to a specific region, which is the case for Cognac as well as for Armagnac. Something these spirits have in common is the fact that they are based on wine, which is often sour and unpleasant to drink undistilled. Pot stills are often used in the manufacturing process, but also column stills. Two examples of this are Cognac and Armagnac respectively, where the latter is often distilled in a continuous process in simple column stills.

Both French classics require aging in oak casks. The purpose of this is that the casks add, take away and cause interaction between different components. The final product is smoother, with flavours of vanilla, oak, coconut or arrack and spicy, sweet and nutty notes. One of the main differences compared with whisky is that casks are often exchanged during aging. As maturing proceeds, casks are shifted a couple of times to diminish the effect of the cask on the distillate. This is done as a result of the first casks being fresher and thus providing stronger notes of oak, spices, vanilla and so on. After a few years, the maturing environment is exchanged for casks that have already been used, and thereby are more washed out. It allows the spirit to mature in an environment that has less effect on the now smoother spirit. When the maturing process is longer, this can occur in several steps. It thus differs from whisky, which stays in the same cask throughout the maturing process. The colouring and sweetening of brandy is allowed, and is used, as with whisky, especially for simpler and cheaper sorts.

Age in the world of brandy is described by means of a number of not entirely standardised systems. No less than two years of aging in oak casks is required. The minimum age requirements are set according to the Compte system:

Three star, VS/de luxe: 3–4 years
VO, VSOP: 5–6 years
XO, Extra: 7–8 years

Please note, however, that many manufacturers are more generous in their classifications than the system demands. A VS is usually aged 3–5 years, a Napoleon 7–15 years and an XO 20–25 years.

COGNAC

Cognac is the best-known type of brandy in the world and the one that can be aged the longest, thanks to the soil in the area of origin. The character of cognac varies depending on the ambitions and goals of the manufacturers. Younger cognac is generally speaking more fiery, with grape notes and it is more perfume-like. With age, it absorbs more of the cask – spiciness, vanilla, coconut, arrack. It also tends to become smoother and softer in the mouth and develop a range of colours that go from hay yellow to dark amber.

ARMAGNAC AND OTHER AGED AND UN-AGED BRANDIES

Even though it might be considered rather mean to the Armagnac, so charming and full of character, we have gathered everything except Cognac under the same heading. The young Armagnac often has a very sharp and fiery tone which, as with other young spirits, still contributes a generous impression of the original vegetal matter. The Armagnac is rather impure, which makes it suitable for long aging, rendering it with awe-inspiring age traits while keeping a spiritual, youthful character of grapes, sultanas and figs.

As mentioned above, column distillation is common for Armagnac. The same method can also be used for other French brandies. Since the simpler sorts are aged for a shorter period, sugar and colouring are added at a later stage of the process.

Outside France, there are many other types of grape distillates. Examples include the caramelly, sweet, grapy and rich Spanish distillates from Jerez and other parts of Spain.

Perhaps you are familiar with other 'burnt' wine products in this spirit category. Several high-quality brands are made in more recent wine producing countries such as South Africa, Australia and the US. You may also have tasted the soapy, perfume-like sweetness of a Greek Metaxa.

Finally, un-aged grape distillates also include pomace brandies. These are called *grappa* in Italy and *marc* (pronounced *maar*) in France. They are simple types of brandy that people either love or hate. Sure, there are matured pomace brandies too, but in that case, why not go for a cognac? The best grappas are often the ones with a lot of character and a dry, prominent taste of grape. Grappa and its peers are made from pressed grape residue – skins, seeds and twigs. You remove the sugar and flavours by steaming or make a mash that is distilled to produce the alcohol that these wine-making leftovers can bring. Grappa and other pomace brandies are often oily, fusel sweet and have noticeable characteristics of the type of grape that is used. There are also typical grape aromas to be found of black pepper, Muscat, chocolate, pencil lead, blackcurrants and, admittedly, a slightly harsh hint of grape seeds.

Grappa is often served as a digestif, an after-dinner drink, perhaps after a sturdy Italian eight-course meal.

CALVADOS
Calvados is a distillate based on apples. However, it often also has a large influence of pears, as this fruit bears flavour well, due to its high acidity. Within the areas where calvados is manufactured, there are different sets of regulations concerning the manufacture. These include Pays d'Auge, where only apples may be used as vegetal matter, and Domfrontais, where at least 30 per cent of the original crop needs to consist of apples.

The name 'calvados' is a protected appellation and may only be used for apple-based brandy from Normandy, France. These brandies are aged in oak casks for a minimum of two years, which may be considered unnecessarily long. True, a 30-year-old calvados may possess an incredibly rich tone of mature apple brandy and damp apple storage rooms filled with ripening apples. But on the other hand, a 'Norman hole' in the stomach in the middle of dinner, a trou Normand, from a calvados of two or three years, is more than refreshing!

OTHER FRUIT SPIRITS
Anyone who has travelled around in the Alps, may find something missing from this survey. This is true – fruit distillates also include the clear, often un-aged and highly crop-intense German, Austrian and Balkan fruit spirits. Obstler, as they are called in German, are made from plums and other fruit such as peaches, pears or anything else that might grow in a blossoming mountain valley and is suitable as a base for spirits.

Whisky and Whiskey
– Scotland, Ireland, Canada and the USA

THE BASICS

Whisky and whiskey are grain-based. Regardless of whether spelt with an 'e' as in Ireland and in the US, or without an 'e', as in Scotland, there are obvious similarities. The type of cereal used in Scotland and Ireland is barley. In Scotland, the barley is malted and in Ireland malted as well as unmalted barley is used. An American bourbon whiskey is based on corn, but also contains barley malt and rye, or wheat. Barley malt, rye and wheat may also be used as the main ingredient, but that means that the label according to US law must include the words malt, rye or wheat whiskey.

In a blended whisky, the industrially made base spirit, the neutral spirit, may have any crop as its starch source. This is broken down into fermentable sugar in the first step of the manufacturing process.

For Scotch malt whiskies, the sugar source is malted barley. Malting entails making the barley germinate and then roasting it, or kiln-drying it, to use the proper whisky and brewing term. If peat is used to fuel the fire during kilning, it contributes a smoky note that evokes coke smoke and tar. The roasted malt is then milled and covered with hot water in the mashing process. With the help of the enzymes in the barley, the starch is then broken down into sugars and leached. The result is a sugar solution called wort. The mashing is followed by fermentation and later distillation.

The final step, before the whisky is ready for bottling, is maturation. The maturation takes place in oak casks made from European or American oak. The main difference between the two is that while the European oak gives more colour, spiciness and complexity, the American contributes with mainly vanilla aromas. The casks used for Scotch are in 95 percent of the cases old bourbon casks. In most other cases, casks that have originally contained sherry are used. There are also casks that once contained other liquids. These are used during the finishing stage, when Scotch is stored in another type of cask for a short period. This is done to spice up the character of, for example, rum, Madeira, port, wine and occasionally even beer.

The maturation time is indicated in legislation. In Europe, the spirit must be aged in oak casks for no less than three years to be allowed to be called whisky or whiskey. In the US, the rule is two years. Additionally, in the US, the label must indicate whether the whiskey is less than four years old.

SCOTCH

Another difference in the production method can be found in the final blending of the products. Ninety percent of all Scotch sold is blended. Blended whisky is made up of plain spirits that have been flavoured with malt whisky. Typically, about a third of the volume consists of 10–20 different types of malt whisky.

Single malt, on the other hand, is a pot still distillate from a single distillery, using only malted barley as vegetal matter. Scottish malt whisky is distilled twice, with few exceptions.

The character of Scotch varies in a way that is comparable to the difference between vodka made from potatoes and potatoes themselves. Blended whiskeys from Scotland keep a tidy, often very mildly smoky and malty, sweet form. Single malt, on the other hand, can be found in everything from flowery, unsmoked lowland whiskies to fat malty and rich Speysides as well as the extremes: smoky, peaty and tar-like Islay.

IRISH WHISKEY

Large amounts of unmalted barley is added to Irish whiskey. This has a historical explanation:

malted barley used to be taxed more heavily than unmalted. For the past decades, Irish whiskey has been unsmoked, triple-distilled and with a great dominance of bourbon casks used in aging. Most Irish whiskies are blended, but there is also something called 'pure pot still', which can be compared to the Scottish malt whisky.

Apart from the traits mentioned above, the character of Irish whiskey is also often mild, creamy, sweet and malty. The dominance of bourbon cask aging results in a distinctive but mild oak tone with a great part of vanilla, and a characteristic scent reminiscent of geraniums, black currant leaves, or, according to some ungenerous judges, cat pee …

AMERICAN WHISKEY

Regulations require one main crop to be used for each type of American whiskey. For bourbon it is corn, for malt malted barley, rye for rye and wheat for wheat whiskey.

American whiskey is generally a lot fruitier, more caramelly and lighter, perhaps more perfume-like, than Scotch. American whiskies often have stronger oak aromas, which lend a supreme balance to the sweeter, fruiter ingredients in, above all, bourbon.

The characteristics of American whiskey can mainly be explained by the vegetal matter, but also the fact that American manufacturers by law are compelled to use brand new casks. Generally, whiskey is produced in simple column stills combined with a subsequent distillation in a second step, in a still that is rather like a pot still. Together, there two steps result in a distinctive neutral spirit well worth aging.

As an aside, we might just mention Tennessee whiskey. Until the neutral spirit is ready, the same principles as for bourbon apply when it comes to ingredients and production technique. According to regulations, Tennessee whiskey is filtered through ten feet deep beds of sugar-maple charcoal before it is put in casks for aging. This procedure adds a faint extra sweetness and softness to the distillate as the sharpest edges of the plain spirit are polished off. There are only two distillers left in Tennessee today, Jack Daniel's and George Dickel.

CANADIAN, JAPANESE AND OTHER WHISKIES

Canada is a big country when it comes to whisky production, at least in terms of volume. Canadian whisky is generally a very mild, neutral spirit, which gets its character from a humble blend of a few percent of pot still distillate, even a small amount of fruit juice is allowed as a flavour enhancer.

Japan is another major whisky producing country. Most of it has until recent years been sold on the domestic market only. Japanese whisky is generally of a very high quality and is fully comparable to Scotch, even to malt whisky. Describing the character in only a few words will fail to do it justice, but an attempt may sound like this: high quality, well-balanced between rich maltiness, mild smokiness and occasionally a hint of bitter fruitiness.

In addition to the countries mentioned above, whisky is manufactured in many parts of the world including Sweden, Finland, England, Australia, Germany, Austria and Switzerland. The scent and flavour of these are best explored on a well-stocked whisky fair. Cheers to a Swissky!

LIQUEURS

Liqueurs are rather like herb spirits. They are based on a distillate – vodka, brandy or whisky – and the flavourings vary from herbs and spices in, for example, Jägermeister to fruit and berries in cherry, orange, melon and other liqueurs. Other common flavourings include nuts, chocolate, coffee beans, milk and eggs. A clear definition of a liqueur is that it is a spirit that contains more than 100 grams of sugar per litre. The difference between liqueur and spirits is quite difficult to explain today, when many spirits are flavoured (vodka, for example). But the sweetness constitutes a clear difference, as well as the fact that the liqueur usually only contains about 15–30 per cent alcohol (although some contain up to 55 per cent). Dessert wines may taste like liqueurs, but contains no added flavourings, nor are they manufactured by means of distillation but through fermentation, like all wines.

The name 'liqueur' comes from the Latin expression *liquifacere*, meaning 'to condense'. This relates to the distillation process, which is something the liqueur has in common with other spirits. Not surprisingly, considering the Anglo-American words 'liqueur' and 'liquor' respectively.

SPARKLING WINE

This survey of basic cocktail ingredients focuses on spirits. However, many cocktails contain a low-alcohol ingredient, sparkling wine. Much like the fame of brandy among after-dinner drinks, the French champagne has a top of mind status among bubblies.

Sparkling wines are exported by more or less all wine-producing countries. Champagne is a well-known example, but there are other French sparkling wines, so called *crémant*, as well as Spanish cava and Italian *spumante*.

Sparkling wines can be produced in a few different ways, at different costs and with different results. The most basic method is to make a wine and then carbonate it — the so-called soft drinks method. A second method is to make the wine and then keep it in a bulk tank at low temperature (a few degrees Celsius), and adding yeast and sugar to achieve the carbonation. After this step, the yeast residue is filtered away and the wine is bottled. Slow fermentation at a low temperature gives the wine a higher quality in terms of retained grape character and creamy, long-lasting bubbles.

The third method is the so called champagne method whereby a mixture of yeast and sugar is added in connection with the bottling of the white wine. As fermentation proceeds and bubbles start to appear, the bottles are turned from a horizontal to an upside-down position. After fermentation is completed, the neck of the bottle is frozen and the lees are forced out as a result of the high pressure. Before the wine is ready for bottling, and goes on either to aging or straight to the shops, it can sometimes benefit from further sweetening or addition of wine.

By Örjan Westerlund

The History of Spirits

In short, distilling means adding energy in order to separate one liquid in a mix from another. This is only possible if the liquids have different boiling points. It is likely that humans have known this for a very long time, at least in practice. There is documented evidence that we have been familiar with the principles of distillation since the cradle of human culture – in Mesopotamia around 3500 BC the distillation method was used for making perfumes.

All the way back in ancient Egypt, people enjoyed themselves with distillation when they were not out building pyramids. Using alchemy, attempts were made to separate the four elements. These skills were spread both northward to the Greeks and eastward to China and India. There is documentation of distillation having taken place in India as early as 800 BC.

With the spread of the new knowledge, medical science in Europe began to practice distillation. The art of distillation came to us in the Western world via monks and crusaders returning from the Middle East, where they had picked up this art from the moors. The pilgrims conveyed the knowledge to doctors and other professionals, for example gunpowder manufacturers. The first documented evidence of distillation in Europe dates back to the middle of the 12th century, from the faculty of medicine at the University of Salerno, Italy.

At the very beginning of the 14th century, professor of medicine Arnault de Villeneuve coined the expression eau de vie, water of life. In his alchemic experiments, he and his colleagues searched for a fifth element – the *quinta essentia*. He believed himself to have found this very thing in alcohol, a substance that gives life and power and, as he believed, could be used in the production of gold. His own words about the elixir he discovered were that it 'prolongs life, gets rid of bad temper, rejuvenates the heart and keeps man young'.

As quickly as a rumour, the discovery that alcohol was good for internal use started to spread. There are several examples that testify that people took Arnault's credo about the water of life literally. It was regarded as a remedy for most troubles: gout, lice and toothache as well as bad temper and, later on, even alcoholism. Naturally, the horrific plague of the mid 14th century was one of the diseases believed to be best cured with the water of life.

During late medieval times, people were more and more often seen staggering about towns and parishes as a consequence of private medication and plain boozing. The local authorities were forced to handle the consequences of this behaviour. As a result, plans were soon made for the limitation and regulation of the production and consumption of alcohol.

INVENTION OF NEW MANUFACTURING PRINCIPLES

In the beginning of the 18th century, as a result of the industrial revolution, British manufacturers began striving for a more industrialised spirit manufacturing process. However, complicated regulations made legal production difficult. Scottish producers, who succeeded in manufacturing great volumes of un-aged spirits, sold their products to England where it was made into gin. Generally, in other countries too, the manufacture originally took place in pot stills. These were simple, built-over pots which were heated from underneath. The steam from the mash was collected in the 'swan's neck' that lead from the lid. It was later chilled, often in a spiral cooler, before dripping down from the cooler in the form of a more highly concentrated alcoholic condensate.

The development of the production methods eventually led to the British invention of the so called column still in the early 19th century (read more about this and the pot still on page 23). After a few less functional models, the design of this still was improved considerably. This led to a working principle which is widely used to this day. It was patented in 1830 by Aeneas Coffey. This Irishman and former tax commissioner had thus created the foundation for the industrial manufacture of commercial spirits. In this continuous process, any type of crop containing starch could be boiled, mashed and then distilled into a spirit of very high purity. The disadvantages of the old-fashioned pot still principle were now gone with the wind. However, the column still had one great disadvantage: the spirit was pure, and therefore neutral and flavourless. Attempts at aging this spirit did not quite work. The pot still whisky, on the other hand, had a rustic and expressive character.

BLENDING DIFFERENT SPIRITS

The qualities of each manufacturing principle were taken advantage of in what has become the world's best selling type of whisky today. In fact, there are other types of spirits where pot still and column still spirits are mixed together, rum and brandy, for example, as this provides a balance between the various desirable qualities of the components.

Blended whisky began to appear in the mid 19th century. The credit for this invention normally goes to a shopkeeper in Perth by the name of Andrew Usher. He, or more likely his wife, came up with the idea of spicing up neutral column pot spirits with distinctive malt whiskies from their suppliers.

The benefits came rushing in like coins in a slot machine: blended whisky was cheap due to its content of column still spirits, it was rich in flavour and aroma thanks to the malt whisky, and, not least, it could be designed according to personal taste. Every shopkeeper could now make his own type of whisky. You could achieve exactly the level of smokiness, sweetness and richness the customers desired. The genius of it was also that one ingredient in the recipe could be replaced with a similar one, should the quality or supply be insufficient.

PHYLLOXERA AND BRANDY DROUGHT

The timing for this invention within the world of whisky was excellent. Within the British Empire, there was access to a worldwide trade, which could be conducted 'nationally'. At the time when blending first started, there was a possibility of taking pleasure in the misfortunes of the French, as French vineyards were attacked by the Phylloxera pest. As a result of inadequate routines in the quarantine process, the pest struck vineyards starting from the late 1850s, after grapevines that had been contaminated with the *Phylloxera vastatrix* had been brought over from the US. The second part of the name means 'the destroyer'. In 1872, the wine growing in the Charente region was knocked out. With no wine growing in the area where cognac is made, no cognac could be made.

BRANDING AND FAILED PROHIBITION TEETOTALISM

The spread of whisky is to a great extent typical of the well-known spirit brands, which were disseminated, beginning in the last decades of the 19th century, by active entrepreneurs in an expanding world trade, with great help from clever marketing of the new trademarks. Some examples of faithful old servants from this period are Johnnie Walker and Jack Daniel's as well as Hennessy, Pernod and Fernet-Branca.

The increased popularity of strong spirits in the early 19th century brought the debate into issues of public health and restrictions. A temperance movement developed as the drinking curse became more and more apparent. During the early 20th century, the discussions became more animated. As a result, prohibition and a moratorium on manufacture were introduced in some American states and parts of Europe before and during WW1.

In the US, the Prohibition era came to an end when Roosevelt was elected president. The Great Depression and the Prohibition were obvious reasons for his famous words in connection with the repeal of the Prohibition in 1933: 'What America needs now is a drink!'

HISTORY OF THE COCKTAIL

The word 'cocktail' was most likely mentioned for the first time in 1803 in the *Farmer's Cabinet* newspaper. The word in itself has no certain explanation. One theory is that the term could derive from a distortion of the French word for eggcup, *coquetier*, which would in that case relate to the serving measures. Another theory points to a humorous paraphrase of the Latin word for 'watery', decoctus. A perhaps less probable explanation is the theory that feathers were sometimes used for garnishing drinks. A more practical explanation originates from the English language and may be considered more likely due to its everyday connection – drinks were often made from the heeltaps of, for example, cognac casks. The drops were called 'tailings' and came out of a 'stop cock'.

A milestone in the history of cocktails is the 1862 book *Bartender's Guide: How to Mix Drinks* by Jerry Thomas. Some of the cocktails we still like to order today, sours and slings, for example, can be found in this book. Regardless of the origin of the word, an early starting point for cocktail-mixing was the combination of sweet flavours with sour and bitter ones. A classic example is the Old Fashioned, which came into being when a customer, Colonel James E. Pepper, expressed his dislike for the taste of whiskey. He asked the bartender of his favourite hangout, the Pendennis Club, in the heart of bourbon–making Kentucky, to disguise the whiskey flavour. The bartender did this elegantly by muddling a sugar cube with bitter angostura drops and a bit of soda water. He then blended rye whiskey with ice, and camouflaged the whiskey flavour even more by finishing off his creation with a slice of orange – sweet, bitter and sour in a pleasant balance.

Since the turn of the 20th century, which was when this well-known recipe was composed, the drink culture has exploded. There have been some significant setbacks, such as the Prohibition era, but even during that period the lack of high-quality ingredients caused a burst of creativity. After Prohibition, and as a result of American culture spreading throughout the world, drinks and cocktails became everyman's property, and with it came an almost infinite number of creative names for new and old recipes that prescribed countless flavours, colours and garnishes.

Legendary Cocktail Bars Around the World

HARRY'S BAR
Venice, Italy

This is where the divine, peach-flavoured champagne cocktail known as Bellini was created. It is to this day made from fresh white peaches according to the original recipe, and has been sipped by celebrities for 60 years.

Harry's is one of the world's oldest and most legendary cocktail bars. Over the past decades, it has been the favourite hangout of the rich and famous: Marilyn Monroe, Orson Welles, Charlie Chaplin and Katherine Hepburn to mention a few. Ernest Hemingway worked on his book Across the River and Into the Trees at one of the little round wooden tables. The bar is as just as popular, if not more popular, today with famous frequenters like Nicole Kidman, Helen Hunt and Richard Gere. Woody Allen held his wedding dinner at Harry's, which, despite its prime status as a bar, also has a star in the Guide Michelin.

In 1929, hotel bartender Giuseppe Cipriani rather apprehensively lends a young, unhappy regular all his savings. The young man has fallen from his rich family's grace, which makes him unable to afford a ticket back to America. A year later, when Giuseppe begins to think that the money has been lost forever, the young American steps into the hotel with a huge stack of banknotes, which he hands over to Giuseppe with the words: 'Thanks for the loan, and for the rest of the money, we're going to open a bar named Harry's.' The rest is history. Giuseppe's son, Arrigo (the Italian version of Harry), now runs Harry's in the same spirit as his father once did. The success and legendary status of the bar depends on the family's business concept – to treat everyone alike – and to treat them as royalty. Something which may not always be appreciated by royalties themselves, who have to wait their turn like everybody else …

San Marco 1323, 301 24 Venice, Italy
+ 39 41 528 5777, www.harrysbarvenezia.com

LONG BAR
Raffles Hotel, Singapore

One of the world's most famous and exclusive luxury hotels, Raffles Hotel, built in 1887, is one of Singapore's greatest sights. For the cocktail lover, however, the hotel bar is the most interesting part. Here, a piece of female emancipation history was made in the shape of the cocktail Singapore Sling.

The year was 1915. Singapore was under British colonial rule and it was generally considered vulgar for women to have a drink. Until then, a drink had chiefly meant whisky or brandy, either 'on the rocks' or mixed with something sour such as tonic or lime – it was all male territory. Ngiam Tong Boon, bartender at Raffles Hotel, found this unfair and wanted a change. After much experimenting with fruit juices he created a sweet mixture, low in alcohol, which soon became very popular among high society ladies. Suddenly, a woman gliding around with a female pink Singapore Sling in her hand was regarded as a woman of style and taste, and this quickly spread all the way back to England. Bartenders all over the world followed suit and started to create a multitude of new, sweet cocktails – the modern long drink trend was born.

In the same white, charming British colonial style hotel, it is to this day possible to lounge in the dark brown rattan chairs surrounded by huge green palm trees, sipping a 'sling'. As a snack, customers can order unpeeled peanuts whose shells they are expected to throw straight on the floor – a curious tradition that might be hard to adopt. The crunching of the shells under your feet is supposed to remind you of dry leaves inside the houses at the old plantations.

Singapore Sling is one of the most complicated cocktails to get right due to the long list of ingredients. The recipe has also undergone some changes over the years. The latest version is from around 1970, and was created by a nephew of Ngiam Tong Boon's. The hotel has its own museum, where one of the original recipes can be seen behind glass, and also the safe where Ngiam Tong Boon kept his recipes.

Raffles Hotel, 1 Beach Road, Singapore 189673, +65 6337 1886, www.raffles.com

THE BAR HEMINGWAY
Hôtel Ritz, Paris, France

Built in the early years of the 19th century as a palace, the Hôtel Ritz is one of the most beautiful and luxurious hotels in the world. World leaders and royalties such as King Edward VII and the shah of Iran have stayed there, and so has Greta Garbo, Marlene Dietrich, Maurice Chevalier and Charlie Chaplin. Coco Chanel may possess the record – she stayed at the hotel for over 30 years! Ernest Hemingway, a frequent bar customer, had a whole bar named after him to be on the safe side.

In the Bar Hemingway, customers recline in leather armchairs surrounded by wood panelling and other authentic props that lend it the right atmosphere from the days when old Papa himself used to sit there. The hotel has been particularly good at attracting authors, who can even have their mail forwarded, a tradition unique to the Ritz. Literary giants such as James Joyce, Graham Greene and Jean-Paul Sartre have found inspiration there. And should you get tired of Hemingway, why not try one of the other 3 or 4 bars? Velvet, silk, gold, great floral arrangements and white garden statues. It is as fancy as it could be.

Hôtel Ritz, 15 Place Vendôme, 75001 Paris, France, +33 01 43 16 30 30, www.ritzparis.com

HARRY'S NEW YORK BAR
Paris, France

It is said to be the birthplace of the Bloody Mary cocktail, although the King Cole Bar is another contestant for the origin of the tomato-based drink. At the time, around the 1920s, there was a bartender working there by the name of Fernand 'Pete' Petiot. When he moved to New York and brought with him the tradition of mixing spirits with tomato juice – which was not uncommon in Europe at the time –the cocktail got its big breakthrough, with the help of a few spices …

Apart from the Bloody Mary, owner Harry McElhone was a constant reinventor of drinks – every occasion called for a new and special cocktail. White Lady, Sidecar, The Blue Lagoon and a whole bunch of other drinks are said to be his creations (even though a certain Harry Craddock also claims copyright for the White Lady, but possibly with the original crème de menthe instead of gin).

The story of Harry's begins in 1911 when an American former star jockey Tod Sloan buys an old bistro and names it the 'New York Bar'. He hires a young, Scottish bartender, Harry McElhone, to run it. Sloan's plan is to make money by attracting the American celebrity elite visiting Europe by exploiting his own fame and thus make the bar a financial success. He succeeds, but Sloan's own extravagant lifestyle puts him so deeply into debt that he is forced to sell the bar in 1923. Harry, who after a few years at other bars around the world returns to Paris, realises that his childhood dream of having a bar of his own is within reach, and acts without hesitation. The bar adopts an additional name, 'Harry's' (which has no relation either to Harry's Bar in Venice or to the famous bartender Harry Craddock at the London Savoy Hotel). Harry is a popular owner who does everything to entertain his customers, who love him. When he advertises in a French newspaper he states 'Sank Roo Doe Noo' as the address in order to help Americans make themselves understood in a French taxi. Even more (American) guests follow suit. One of them is George Gershwin, who composes his world-famous musical An American in Paris (which later became a motion picture starring Gene Kelly) in Harry's piano bar.

Harry's is run by the McElhone family to this day. They ensure that the bar remains the same jolly, friendly place that it has always been. There is a piano bar that stays open late and a lunch menu during daytime. New cocktails are added from time to time in Harry's own spirit …

5 Rue Daunou, 75002 Paris, France
+33 01 42 67 71 14, www.harrys-bar.fr

21 CLUB
New York, USA

This is one of the few so-called speakeasies that first made their appearance during the Prohibition era. Cousins Jack Kreindler and Charlie Berns ran this bar at a number of different locations in New York City, under different names. Despite numerous police raids they always managed to move the bar to a new address, sometimes literally bottle by bottle. In some places, they even had reversible shelves, which made it possible to hide the bottles by reversing them to face the wall.

Since 1922, the 21 Club has been loved by the countless number of celebrities that have had their own favourite tables ready for them to book. US presidents such as Jimmy Carter and George Bush Sr preferred table no 7, TV host Larry King and movie star Helen Hayes liked no 2 while Frank Sinatra picked no 14 as his regular table. Over the years, both restaurant and bar have appeared regularly in films and literature: Michelle Pfeiffer and George Clooney made the lounge famous in One Fine Day. In Wall Street, this is where Michael Douglas tries to teach Charlie Sheen about refined food culture. And further back in time, the 21 Club appears in films starring Humphrey Bogart, Roger Moore, Lauren Bacall, Bette Davies, Orson Welles, Ginger Rogers, Tony Curtis and many more.

Among its greatest tourist attractions are the multi-coloured jockey statuettes that parade above the entrance. They are dressed in their team colours and are gifts from stable owners who used to frequent the bar. The interior is full of history; it contains various antiquities, old toys and curiosities which have been donated over the years, each with a symbolic meaning.

The bar has several levels for drinking and eating, the 'Upstairs at 21' being the perfect romantic venue for a proposal. But only if the man first finds himself a blazer, a strict dress code applies.

21 West 52nd Street, New York City, NY 10019, USA, +1 212 582-7200, www.21club.com

THE AMERICAN BAR
The Savoy Hotel, London, England

The building dates back to 1246 when Henry III built the Savoy Palace, but the five-star Savoy hotel we know today opened in 1889. The hotel bar opened in that same year, but was renamed 'The American Bar' in 1930, like many other European bars at the time. The name signalled that new, fashionable American cocktails were served there. They contained juice and soft drinks, and were not merely highly alcoholic mixtures of different spirits, which used to be the case. To mix these beauties, one of the world's most acclaimed bartenders was hired. Harry Craddock, legend has it, was the man behind, for example, White Lady (the version made with crème de menthe). The Savoy Cocktail Book was published the same year. It included a recipe collection signed Harry himself. (New editions of the book have been published over the years with the help of new generations of totally dedicated bartenders working at the hotel, the most recent was published in 1999.)

The bar soon became the number one cocktail bar in London and a favourite hangout of the in-crowd of the time: Judy Garland, Frank Sinatra, Fred Astaire, Marilyn Monroe, John Wayne and Humphrey Bogart – the list is endless. The hotel retains its popularity today, and reopened in 2010 after more than two years of restorations. Innovations include the Savoy Grill headed by celebrity chef Gordon Ramsay. It is probably safe to say that the cocktails are as delicious as they have always been …

Strand, London WC2R 0EU, United Kingdom, +44 20 7836 4343, www.the-savoy.com

KING COLE BAR
The St Regis Hotel, New York, USA

One of New York's most fashionable hotels is located right in the middle of Manhattan. It has everything you could expect from timeless elegance: glittery chandeliers and candelabras, enormous floral arrangements, shiny marble staircases, a brandy lounge and a library with leather sofas as well as a staff who, according to a century-old tradition, tend to the customers' slightest needs. A hotel of this calibre certainly creates high expectations of its bar, and the King Cole Bar indeed has everything: impeccable service, perfect cocktails and – of course – an impressive story to go with it. This is where the Bloody Mary first got truly bloody …

In 1932, Fernand 'Pete' Petiot, the man behind the recipe for the famous tomato drink, moved from Paris to New York City and started to work at the King Cole Bar. Legend has it that the hotel management wanted to avoid swearing, so the Bloody Mary had to be named 'Red Snapper' instead. More ingredients, Tabasco sauce, for example, were later added to the concoction, and the recipe found its way to other circles of bartenders under its original name. Today, there are numerous varieties of the old classic, which can be tried out at the bar. They are the result of years of bartender experience and customer requests.

As a bonus, there is a highly acclaimed wall painting by famous artist Maxwell Parrish over the bar that features a motif that gave the bar its name: Old King Cole (from the classic English nursery rhyme). The mural bears a secret that needs to be coaxed out of the bartender …

2 East 55th Street, NY 10022, USA
+ 1 212 753 45 00, www.stregis.com

EL FLORIDITA
Havana, Cuba

El Floridita is probably the most famous bar in the world. This is where literary giant and rum lover Ernest Hemingway, used to sip the bar's specialty – Daiquiri.

He lived, wrote and met up with his compatriots there. El Floridita's location is perfect for attracting visitors who are just arriving in town, which is something of which Mr Hemingway took advantage. Big-shot businessmen, politicians and most of the celebrities who visited or lived in Cuba could be found here, including many of Hollywood's biggest stars: Errol Flynn, Ava Gardner, Gary Cooper and John Wayne. After he won the Nobel Prize in 1954, a bust was placed above his favourite chair in his honour. Visitors to the El Floridita restaurant today, not only come to drink the delicious Daiquiris and try the delicious Cuban seafood, but also to inhale the atmosphere and mystique from the days of old Papa. He liked his Daiquiris double, and preferably with breakfast, according to a special recipe he put together with the help of El Floridita's own Constantino Ribalaigua, the legendary man behind the epithet 'the King of Cuban bartenders'.

Obispo No. 557, esq. a Monserrate,
Habana Vieja, Ciudad de La Habana, Cuba
+53 7 867 1300, www.floridita-cuba.com

LA BODEGUITA DEL MEDIO
Havana, Cuba

Welcome to the home of the Mojito. The feud between the prides of Havana, the rum cocktails Daiquiri and Mojito, continues to this day. It may have involved both of the two bars that made these national cocktails famous. Hemingway is believed to have said, very diplomatically, 'My Mojito in La Bodeguita. My Daiquiri in El Floridita.' His framed quote hangs on a wall in La Bodeguita, which is also covered in autographs from great movie stars and other legendary celebs who have visited the bar over the years. This is the place to sip a Mojito and feel the wings of history.

Do not let appearances deceive you – at first glance it seems like the bar has no more than eight seats. Move past the kitchen and into the courtyard, or scurry upstairs to the spacious upstairs level that contains another bar and kitchen. La Bodeguita is a popular restaurant, and since a Mojito is perfect in the company of Cuban roasted pork, everything is set for a proper night out!

La Bodeguita del Medio, Calle Empedrado
No 226, Ciudad de La Habana, Cuba
+53 7 867 1374, www.labodeguita.com

THE RED SEA STAR
Eilat, Israel

Like a sunken miniature town, this bar is situated at the bottom of the sea, about 70 meters off shore. Someone once called it a miniature Atlantis. It is this mixture of fairy-tale and reality that strikes guests who are seated six meters below the ocean surface, looking through the windows that face all directions at the crystal-blue underwater world outside. A soothing stillness surrounds you while colourful fish and other inhabitants of the ocean swim past you – but the roles have been reversed. The fish are free on the outside while you are inside the 'tank' …

The Red Sea Star was built in 1999. It is a 'green project' created with the aim of protecting and caring for the surrounding coral reef. There is a specially designed restaurant and bar designed like a colourful cartoon. The Underwater Observatory is open every day of the year between 10 am and 1 am. The water is gently illuminated at night to avoid disturbing the residents of the ocean.

Underwater Observatory, The Southern Square, Eilat, Israel, +972-8-634-777,
www.redseastar.com

B018
Beirut, Lebanon

Is this judgment day? Moonraker? Or Star Wars? Like something constructed by a mad, evil scientist, this architectonic masterpiece lies in wait underground. When night falls, it changes shape and opens up to the sky. The tables are square, the sofas look like coffins and the whole night club is built below ground.

Rather than hiding the fact that Beirut once was a city laid to waste by war, the architect, who is well-known locally, has let himself be inspired by history. Macabre? Hardly, this is considered one of the world's coolest bars according to most visitors. Despite the fact that the looks like a bunker, B018 offers visitors a breathtaking view at night thanks to a skylight that overlooks the stars. Sofas can be turned into mini-stages for anyone in the mood for dancing by simply folding down the backs. On weekends, young clubbers flock here to listen to funk and house music. During the week, Gucci-clad A-celebrities hang out here, sipping their Dry Martinis to the accompaniment of mellow jazz. The bar was built in 1998 in memory of the 1976 massacre. It is, despite everything, a glamorous environment that signals: 'we haven't forgotten, but life goes on!'

Lot 317, La Quarantine, Medwar Beirut, Lebanon, +96 3 800 018, www.b018.com

ORBIT BAR
Sydney, Australia

Take the lift to the 47th floor and step out into an über-designed environment inspired by Stanley Kubrick's 2001 – A Space Odyssey, including everything from white chairs and orange carpets to the specially designed staff outfits. This is hardly the main attraction, however. The bar is called 'Orbit' because of the breathtaking view through the glass walls, which stretch from floor to ceiling, and because it rotates at a speed of about one meter per minute. In this way, guests can enjoy a view over the whole of Sydney from their tables during the time it takes to finish a couple of drinks (one complete revolution takes about 1–1.5 hours). The only downside is that the table will be in a different place from where you left it when you return from the restroom …

Summit Restaurant, Level 47, Australia Square, 264 George Street, Sydney NSW, Australia 2000, +61 2 9247 9777,
www.summitrestaurant.com.au

GIMLET
Barcelona, Spain

This bar is named after hard-boiled crime investigator Philip Marlowe's favourite cocktail, and his fans will no doubt feel very much at home in this timeless environment, which permeates everything from music to interior design. The furnishings have been more or less untouched since the bar opened in the early 1950s.

You are unlikely to bump into any tourists here, but you are bound to encounter a bunch of middle- and upper-class Spanish bohemians instead. There is no use trying to locate Gimlet before 10 pm, since the bar sign will be hidden behind the security grille.

Santaló 46, 08021 Barcelona, Spain,
+34 92 201 53 06, www.gimletbcn.com

ABSOLUT ICE BAR
Jukkasjärvi, Sweden

This is probably Northern Europe's most spectacular bar. Absolut Ice Bar had its grand opening in 1994 as part of the ice hotel. Its whole interior is made out of ice from the nearby Torne River: wall paintings, walls, barstools, beds – the works. The inside temperature is always -5°C, no more, no less. Watch out so you do not get your tongue stuck – even the cocktail glasses are made of ice.

Not surprisingly, every conceivable kind of cocktail made with Absolut Vodka is served here, and walking around this dreamlike ice-world among beautiful ice sculptures and ice chandeliers is like being at a cocktail party in the palace of the Ice Queen. The concept has been highly successful: today, Swedish ice bars can be found all over the world, constructed with blocks of ice from the Torne River. Since ice is short-lived, both hotels and bars must be rebuilt every season, and famous architects and designers fight over who gets to design this year's edition of the world's – no doubt about it – coolest hotel.

Marknadsvägen 1, 981 91 Jukkasjärvi, Sweden
+ 46 980-66 800, www.icehotel.com

'No animal ever invented anything as bad
as drunkenness – or as good as drink.'
Gilbert Keith Chesterton 1874–1936

More Cocktail Bars Around the World

AUSTRIA

Loos Bar, Vienna
www.loosbar.at

CANADA

CN Tower, Toronto
www.cntower.ca

DENMARK

NASA, Copenhagen
www.nasa.dk

Ruby, Copenhagen
www.rby.dk

FRANCE

Experimental Cocktail Club, Paris

The Clubhouse, Chamonix
www.clubhouse.fr

GERMANY

Bar Alexander, Düsseldorf
www.bar-alexander.com

Bogletti, Düsseldorf
www.bogletti.com

Green Door Bar, Berlin
www.greendoor.de

Harry´s New York Bar Esplanade, Berlin
www.esplanade.de

King Kamehameha Club, Frankfurt
www.king-kamehameha.de

Le Lion, Hamburg
www.lelion.net

Schumann's Bar, Munich
www.schumanns.de

Solar, Berlin
www.solarberlin.com

Victoria Bar, Berlin
www.victoriabar.de

T-o12, Stuttgart
www.t-o12.com

ITALY

Harry's Bar, Venice
www.harrysbarvenezia.com

THE NETHERLANDS

Door 74, Amsterdam
www.door74.nl

ROMANIA

Club Embryo, Bucarest
www.embryo.ro

Pat Club, Bucarest
www.inpat.ro

SPAIN

Boadas, Barcelona

Carpe Diem, Barcelona
www.carpediem.es

Dry Martini Bar, Barcelona
www.drymartinibcn.com

Teatriz, Madrid

The Penthouse, Madrid
www.memadrid.com

SWEDEN

Cadierbaren, Grand Hôtel, Stockholm
www.grandhotel.se

First Hotel Reisen, Stockholm
www.firsthotels.com

UNITED KINGDOM

Apartment, Belfast
www.apartmentbelfast.com

Bar Bacca, Belfast
www.barbacca.com

Danger of Death, London
www.dangerlondon.com
MEMBERS ONLY

Duke's Bar, London
www.dukeshotel.com

Mahiki, London
www.mahiki.com

Milk & Honey, London
www.mlkhny.com
MEMBERS ONLY or RESERVATION

Montgomery Place Bar, London
www.montgomeryplace.co.uk

Sketch, London
www.sketch.co.uk

The Blue Bar, Berkeley Hotel, London
www.the-berkeley.co.uk

The Cuckoo Club, London
www.thecuckooclub.com

The Dorchester, London
www.thedorchester.com

The Player, London
www.thplyr.com
MEMBERS ONLY

Vertigo 42, London
www.vertigo42.co.uk

The Starland Social Club, London
www.strlnd.com
MEMBERS ONLY

USA

Angel's Share, New York

Apotheke, New York
www.apothekebar.com

B Flat, New York
www.bflat.info

Campbell Apartment, New York
www.hospitalityholdings.com

Carousel Bar, New Orleans
www.hotelmonteleone.com

Death & Co, New York
www.deathandcompany.com

Drink, Boston
www.drinkfortpoint.com

East Side Company Bar, New York

Eight Lounge, Dallas
www.eightlounge.com

Employees Only, New York
www.employeesonlynyc.com

Flatiron Lounge, New York
www.flatironlounge.com

Florida Room, Miami
www.delano-hotel.com

Hudson Bar, New York
www.hudsonhotel.com

Little Branch, New York

Mad46, The Roosevelt Hotel, New York
www.mad46.com

Mayahuel, New York
www.mayahuelny.com

Milk & Honey, New York
www.mlkhny.com

Morimoto, New York
www.morimotonyc.com

Painkiller, New York
www.painkillernyc.com

PDT (Please don't tell), New York
www.pdtnyc.com

Pegu Club, New York
www.peguclub.com

Purdy Lounge, Miami
www.purdylounge.com

Rain in the Desert, Las Vegas
www.n9negroup.com

Rainbow Room, New York
www.cipriani.com

S Bar, Los Angeles
www.sbe.com

Skybar, Los Angeles
www.mondrianhotel.com

Star Lounge, New York
www. starloungechelsea.com

Studio 54, Las Vegas
www.mgmgrand.com

The Empire Room, Empire State Building,
New York

The Varnish, Los Angeles
www.thevarnishbar.com

CHINA

Antidote, Hong Kong

Aqua, Hong Kong
www.aqua.com.hk

Cloud 9, Shanghai
www.shanghai.grand.hyatt.com

LAN Club Oyster Bar, Beijing
www.lanbeijing.com

Mo Bar, Hong Kong
www.mandarinoriental.com

Peninsula Hotel Oyster Bar, Hong Kong
www.peninsula.com

Tou Ming Si Kao (TMSK), Shanghai
www.tmsk.com

Volar, Shanghai

JAPAN

Absolut Icebar, Tokyo
www.icebartokyo.com

Club Camellia, Hiroshima

THAILAND

Bamboo Bar, Bangkok
www.mandarinoriental.com/bangkok

Supperclub, Bangkok
www.bedsupperclub.com

The Dome, Bangkok
www.thedomebkk.com

Vertigo, Bangkok

SINGAPORE

New Asia Bar
www.swissotel.com

LEBANON

Crystal, Beirut

UNITED ARAB EMIRATES

Vu's Bar, Dubai
www.jumeirahemiratestowers.com

AUSTRALIA

Bond Lounge Bar, Melbourne
www.bondlounge.com.au

Orbit Bar, Sydney
www.summitrestaurant.com.au

The Loft, Sydney
www.theloftsydney.com

NEW ZEALAND

Crow Bar, Auckland
www.crowbar.co.nz

SOUTH AFRICA

Planet Bar, Mount Nelson Hotel, Cape Town
www.mountnelson.co.za

MEXICO

La Capilla, Tequilla

COCKTAILS

We have been enjoying mixed drinks in everything from buzzing city cellar bars and the lobby bars of the great hotels to sun-drenched beach bars in every tropical paradise on the planet. We are grateful to the American prohibition, which gave us the abundance of cocktails and mixed drinks that were created during this period and that are still with us today. Secret underground bars and speakeasies emerged, in which the beautiful people of the 1920s and 30s could socialise without having to give up alcohol. Moonshine of various qualities was served there, and sometimes the spirits were barely drinkable. Bartenders were forced to develop a great deal of creativity as they had no choice but to use different sorts of fruit juice and other mixers in order to disguise the taste of fusel. This brand new mixed drink suddenly became trendy, and 'American bars' began to pop up in Europe too, despite the fact that whisky and gin – both legal and drinkable – could be purchased there.

The origin of the modern-day cocktail, however, dates back to long before the 'Jazz Age'. The following sarcastic comment about cocktails could be read in an American newspaper: 'It [the cocktail] is considered a suitable preparation for democratic presidential candidates, since a person who has had a glass is thereafter prepared to swallow just about anything.' This was in 1806, but the first discernable cocktail, a predecessor of the Cuban classic Mojito, dates all the way back to the 16th century.

Cocktails are mixed drinks made from two or more ingredients. Originally this used to mean distilled spirits of some kind combined with sugar, water and something bitter (like the Old Fashioned). The concept was later developed further, and came to include fruit juices, soda water, milk, cream and herbs. Today, the word 'cocktail' is more of a generic term used to describe all sorts of mixed drinks, but a 'real' cocktail is a short drink served in a high-stemmed glass – a cocktail glass. Hence the name of this book, although a 'cocktail' is merely one category of drinks.

COCKTAIL OR SHORT DRINK?
The first cocktail recipe of this book is found overleaf. Cocktails served in high-stemmed glasses, usually a Martini glass, are included in the category 'Short Drinks'. Other short drinks are usually served in various types of tumblers, on the rocks or with crushed ice. Something that all short drinks have in common, however, is that the alcohol is more concentrated than in the so-called long drinks, which makes them perfect aperitifs.

If served in a stemmed glass, the cocktail is always served without ice, which means that chilling the glass as well as the ingredients is crucial. Read more about this in the sections *Ice*, *Shaking* and *Mixing Glass* earlier in this book. After pouring the drink into the cocktail glass, it should be consumed immediately, while it is still cold. Hold the glass by the stem to avoid warming the contents with your hand.

This category also includes most champagne cocktails, which make excellent aperitifs too, as they signal the start of a great dinner and a fantastic evening ahead!

Bronx

1 ½ oz (45 ml) gin
½ oz (15 ml) red vermouth
½ oz (15 ml) dry vermouth
1 oz (30 ml) orange juice

Pour all the ingredients into
a shaker filled with ice. Shake
well and strain into a chilled
cocktail glass.

TIP! *Use juice from blood oranges
instead, and you have made a
Bloody Bronx.*

*All vermouth is made from white wine. Red vermouth is coloured at the end of the manufacturing
process. Bronx is a 'Perfect Martini' (equal parts red and dry vermouth) laced with orange juice. It was
created as early as in 1906 by Johnny Solon, bartender at the Waldorf Astoria in New York City. Many
other versions of the Dry Martini, the world's no. 1 cocktail, were to follow …*

Cosmopolitan

1 ½ oz (45 ml) lemon vodka
½ oz (15 ml) Cointreau
1 oz (30 ml) cranberry juice
½ oz (15 ml) fresh lime juice

Pour all the ingredients into a shaker filled with ice. Shake well and strain into a chilled cocktail glass.

This cocktail is said to have been created in the San Francisco gay district in the 1980s, but its big breakthrough was in the hit TV-series Sex and the City (it was the favourite cocktail of main character Carrie Bradshaw). In the first spin-off feature film, script writers allude to the fans of the TV-series when they let Miranda ponder over why they ever stopped drinking Cosmos. Carrie replies: 'Because everyone else started.'

Metropolitan

1 ½ oz (45 ml) Absolut Kurant
½ oz (15 ml) Cointreau
1 oz (30 ml) cranberry juice
½ oz (15 ml) lime cordial
Egg white

Pour all the ingredients into
a shaker filled with ice. Shake
well and strain into a chilled
cocktail glass.

TIP! *Hey, Carrie Bradshaw! You've
been drinking the wrong cocktail all
along. It was this drink you should
have been sipping sulkily all those
years when you didn't want to leave
the big city...*

*The name of this cocktail suggests urban nightlife, and it is indeed a relatively young cocktail with a
true New York connection. It is said to have been created in 1993 at Marion's Continental Restaurant
in New York. The theory that the drink was named after The Met opera or the art museum with the
same name is perhaps unlikely. It is more likely a tribute to people in big cities with a certain lifestyle.*

Cucumber Cocktail

2 oz (60 ml) gin
1 oz (30 ml) lemon juice
½ oz (15 ml) simple syrup
1 slice cucumber
1 pinch wasabi

Muddle the cucumber and wasabi gently with sugar syrup in a shaker. Fill up with crushed ice and add gin and lemon juice. Give it a good shake. Strain into a cocktail glass.

Wasabi is known as Japanese horseradish, and has been cultivated there for more than 1,000 years, but it also grows wild along rivers and lakes. The best wasabi grows in running water, and the root is grated using shark's skin rather than a cheese grater. A common ingredient in Japanese dishes, especially those containing fish, wasabi is also rather surprisingly used to flavour ice cream and sweets. Since it is an expensive product, it is often mixed with ordinary horseradish and green food colouring, or simply replaced by it. This 'wasabi' is often used in less exclusive sushi restaurants.

Melon Ball

1 oz (30 ml) lemon vodka
½ oz (15 ml) elderflower
  liqueur
½ oz (15 ml) melon liqueur
Carambola for garnish

Pour all ingredients into a
shaker filled with ice. Shake
well and strain into a chilled
cocktail glass. Garnish with
sliced carambola.

*A 'melon baller' is, unsurprisingly, a tool used for making melon balls in about the same way as we
scoop up ice-cream. This cocktail is probably not named after the tool, more likely after a romantic ball
underneath a starlit night sky …*

Manhattan

1 ½ oz (45 ml) Canadian
  whisky
½ oz (15 ml) red vermouth
2 dashes Angostura bitters
Maraschino cherries for
  garnish

Pour all the ingredients into
a mixing glass with plenty
of ice cubes. Stir well until
chilled. Strain into a chilled
cocktail glass and garnish with
cherries.

TIP! *Use bourbon to make your
Manhattan milder. Use Scotch
instead, and you get a completely
different cocktail – a Rob Roy.*

*The young newly-wed high society girl Jenny Churchill was not only pretty, she was politically minded too.
In 1874, she held a political convention at the Manhattan Club in New York City. As legend has it, she
asked the bartender to create a new cocktail in the honour of newly elected governor Samuel J. Tildens.
Later that year, Jenny gave birth to a baby boy. Both were to become legendary. The cocktail was named
Manhattan and the boy Winston …*

Rob Roy

1 ½ oz (45 ml) Scotch whisky
½ oz (15 ml) red vermouth
1 dash Angostura bitters
Maraschino cherries for garnish

Pour whisky and vermouth into a mixing glass with plenty of ice cubes. Stir well until chilled. Strain into a chilled cocktail glass, add Angostura bitters and garnish with cherries.

Rob Roy is essentially a Manhattan made with Scotch blended whisky instead of bourbon. Originally, it contained equal parts whisky and vermouth. 'Roy' is also what the Scots would call a male redhead. Robert 'Roy' McGregor was a (redhead) Scottish hero with a Robin Hood-like life. Liam Neeson portrayed him in the film Rob Roy, which is set in the early 18th century.

Sidecar

1 oz (30 ml) brandy
1 oz (30 ml) Cointreau
1 oz (30 ml) lemon juice
Maraschino cherries for garnish

Pour all the ingredients into a shaker filled with ice. Shake well and strain into a chilled cocktail glass. Garnish with cherries.

TIP! *For a fuller taste and a more sophisticated feel, use Armagnac instead of plain brandy. Fancy an English Sidecar? Use half the amount of lemon juice and add Cointreau.*

There are several stories explaining the name of this drink. The funniest is the one about an American major in Paris during WW1 who was such a heavy drinker that he constantly had to be brought home in the sidecar of his motor bike.

Bloody Mary Cocktail

1 ½ oz (45 ml) vodka
½ oz (15 ml) sherry
1 oz (30 ml) lemon juice
1 dash Tabasco sauce
1 dash Worcestershire sauce
2 oz (60 ml) tomato juice
¼ tsp celery salt
Black pepper rim and parsley
  for garnish

Pour all the ingredients into a mixing glass with plenty of ice cubes. Stir until chilled. Strain into a chilled martini glass and garnish with parsley.

Black pepper rim?
Pour crushed black pepper onto a saucer. Moisten the rim of the glass with a wedge of lemon and dip the upturned glass into the pepper.

TIP! *Remember to prepare the pepper rim before mixing the drink if you choose to chill the glass in the refrigerator, but afterwards if you chill it by filling it up with ice cubes.*

Here is the world-famous hangover cure in an elegant guise. The original Bloody Mary has been called 'the world's most complex cocktail', but don't let this put you off mixing it!

Between the Sheets

1 oz (30 ml) brandy
½ oz (15 ml) light rum
½ oz (15 ml) Cointreau
½ oz (15 ml) lemon juice

Pour all the ingredients into a shaker filled with ice. Shake well and strain into a chilled cocktail glass.

These silky sheets are rather like a Sidecar, but with a more summery feel. At the end of the American prohibition era, when legal clubs and bars started to reopen, the barkeepers would go to great lengths trying to attract customers, often by creating cocktails with imaginative names. Someone was the inspiration for this seductive drink, but who it was remains uncertain …

Garden

1 oz (30 ml) triple sec
1 oz (30 ml) sour apple liqueur
1 oz (30 ml) passion fruit juice
1 oz (30 ml) lemon juice
½ oz (15 ml) sugar syrup
2 dashes blue curaçao

Pour all the ingredients,
except the curaçao, into a
shaker filled with ice. Shake
well and strain into a chilled
cocktail glass. Trickle the
curaçao over the drink for a
colourful visual effect.

*The passion fruit is actually a berry that is said to relieve asthma. It is a climbing plant that can grow
up to 50 feet tall. The fruit has a dark, brownish purple skin that is smooth when the fruit is fresh.
Maracujá, that has a yellow skin, is another species in the passion flower family.*

Ginger Schnapps

1 oz (30 ml) Absolut Vodka
½ oz (15 ml) lemon liqueur
½ oz (15 ml) lemon juice
½ oz (15 ml) ginger syrup
½ oz (15 ml) peach purée

Pour all the ingredients into a shaker filled with ice. Shake well and strain into a chilled cocktail glass. Garnish with fresh ginger if possible.

Ginger is a hot trend on the cocktail scene today. This cocktail was an entry in a cocktail contest in Sweden, and the name is most likely related to the popular English biscuits ginger snaps.

Green Day

1 oz (30 ml) Irish whiskey
½ oz (15 ml) peach liqueur
½ oz (15 ml) blue curaçao
½ oz (15 ml) orange juice
1 lime wedge
Sugar rim for garnish

Pour all the ingredients into a shaker filled with ice. Shake well and strain into a chilled cocktail glass.

Sugar rim: Pour sugar onto a saucer. Moisten the rim of the glass with the lime wedge and dip the upturned glass into the sugar.

Wear green on March 17 and join in the celebrations of Irish patron saint Patrick! Or celebrate the green island with a tasty green cocktail …

Happy Medium

1 oz (30 ml) spicy dark rum
½ oz (15 ml) vodka
½ oz (15 ml) white chocolate
  liqueur
¼ oz (7 ml) cinnamon syrup

Pour all the ingredients into
a shaker filled with ice. Shake
well and strain into a chilled
cocktail glass. Garnish with a
cinnamon stick.

*In the 1730s, the British Royal Navy introduced a daily ration of rum on board their ships. Gradually,
the ration was diluted with water, which resulted in a drink called 'grog' …*

Ling Gin

2 oz (60 ml) gin
½ oz (15 ml) lemon juice
½ oz (15 ml) sugar syrup
2 tbsp lingonberry or
  cranberry jam

Pour all the ingredients into
a shaker filled with ice. Shake
well and strain into a chilled
cocktail glass.

*This cocktail in named after ex-Playboy playmate Sue Ling Gin. Today, she is a wealthy business woman,
but she started with two empty hands. A journey both sweet and sour, just like this cocktail.*

Green Mist

1 oz (30 ml) whisky
1 oz (30 ml) green crème de menthe
½ oz (15 ml) lemon juice
Egg white

Pour all the ingredients into a shaker filled with ice. Shake well and strain into a chilled cocktail glass.

Irishmen and Americans spell whiskey an 'e', while Scottish whisky is simply called Scotch, or whisky.

Red Baron

2 oz (60 ml) gin
1 oz (30 ml) orange juice
Dash of lemon juice
Dash of Grenadine
Dash of lime juice
Dash of sugar syrup

Pour all the ingredients into a shaker filled with ice. Shake well and strain into a chilled cocktail glass.

This is a sweet, but at the same time tangy, creation named after the German WW1 fighter pilot Manfred von Richthofen. Despite its warlike connotations, this is the perfect cocktail for a hot summer day at the beach.

Japanese Slipper

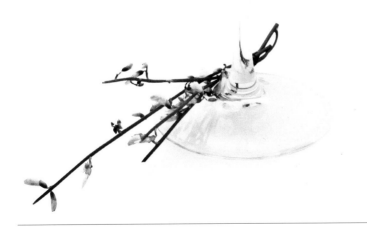

1 oz (30 ml) melon liqueur
1 oz (30 ml) Cointreau
½ oz (15 ml) lemon juice
Melon for garnish

Pour all the ingredients into
a shaker filled with ice. Shake
well and strain into a chilled
cocktail glass. Garnish with a
slice of melon.

*The melon is part of the cucumber family, but is still considered a fruit. Melons have been enjoyed for
thousands of years all over the world and are thought to have originated in Persia.*

Palm Beach

1 ½ oz (45 ml) gin
½ oz (15 ml) sweet vermouth
½ oz (15 ml) grapefruit juice
½ oz (15 ml) pineapple juice
Egg white

Pour all the ingredients into
a shaker filled with ice. Shake
well and strain into a chilled
cocktail glass.

Palm Beach is a popular Florida resort where wealthy celebrities like to build million dollar villas. This famous cocktail has a touch of summery Piña Colada as well as the sophisticated flavours of a Dry Martini – a delicious compromise between two different worlds.

Paradise

2 oz (60 ml) gin
½ oz (15 ml) apricot brandy
1 ½ oz (45 ml) orange juice

Pour all the ingredients into a mixing glass with plenty of ice cubes. Stir well until chilled. Strain into a chilled cocktail glass.

This is a rather unknown cocktail, which has been a beloved aperitif for some time. While a Martini is usually dry, Paradise is sweet and fruity, and perfect as an overture to a lovely summer dinner.

Paradise Mango

1 ½ oz (45 ml) gin
½ oz (15 ml) Passoã Spicy
  Mango
1 ½ oz (45 ml) orange juice

Pour all the ingredients into a
mixing glass with plenty of ice
cubes. Stir well until chilled.
Strain into a chilled cocktail
glass.

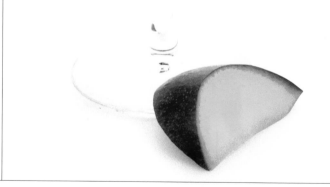

*If you're good, you might get a Paradise cocktail. (But if you're naughty, you might end up somewhere
else where you'll be served tomato juice and Worcestershire sauce in a Bloody Devil cocktail.)*

Pink Lady

2 oz (60 ml) gin
1 oz (30 ml) lemon juice
1 dash grenadine
Egg white

Pour all the ingredients into a shaker filled with ice. Shake well and strain into a chilled cocktail glass.

TIP! *Make the world-famous and mysterious White Lady by replacing grenadine and egg white with ½ oz (15 ml) Cointreau.*

Sweet and innocent? This cocktail has traditionally been labelled a 'girly drink', but appearances can be deceitful. The Pink Lady is a bit cheekier than it seems. In the 1950s, this femininely pink cocktail was said to suit women with little experience of alcohol. The colour suggests fruitiness, but the flavour is more masculine – a rather strong taste of gin and very little sweetness.

Rose

1 oz (30 ml) gin
½ oz (15 ml) dry vermouth
½ oz (15 ml) apricot brandy
½ oz (15 ml) lemon juice
½ oz (15 ml) grenadine

Pour all the ingredients into
a shaker filled with ice. Shake
well and strain into a chilled
cocktail glass.

A romantic English rose for all occasions where a real lady is involved.

Margarita

1 ½ oz (45 ml) tequila
½ oz (15 ml) Cointreau
½ oz (15 ml) lemon or lime juice
1 lemon wedge
Salt rim for garnish

Pour all the ingredients into a shaker filled with ice. Shake well and strain into a chilled margarita glass with a salt rim.

Salt rim: Pour salt onto a saucer. Moisten the rim of the glass with the lemon wedge and dip the upturned glass into the salt.

TIP! *Hold the glass upside-down while moistening the rim to avoid spilling lemon juice all over it.*

This illustrious cocktail may have been named after a certain Margaret Sames, who in 1948 held a Christmas party at her rented villa in Acapulco, Mexico. Among the guests were her friend Elizabeth Taylor with her husband Conrad 'Nicky' Hilton Jr (related to Hilton heiresses Paris and Nicky). This very evening, Ms Sames mixed her favourite liqueur with tequila and lime in order to produce a cocktail with a Mexican touch. Salt and tequila belong together, she thought, and added a salt rim.

Blue Margarita

1 ½ oz (45 ml) tequila
½ oz (15 ml) blue curaçao
½ oz (15 ml) Cointreau
½ oz (15 ml) lime juice
1 lime wedge
Salt or sugar rim for garnish

Pour all the ingredients into a shaker filled with ice. Shake well and strain into a chilled Margarita glass with a salt or sugar rim.

Frosted rim: Pour salt or sugar onto a saucer. Moisten the rim of the glass with the lime wedge and dip the upturned glass into the contents of the saucer.

The name Margarita may have something to do with a certain Mr Pancho, a nervous rookie bartender in Mexico who was asked by a lady customer to mix a 'Magnolia'. He didn't dare admit that he wasn't sure what she was talking about, but he had a vague recollection of something including orange liqueur, so he simply added two of his own favourites, tequila and lime. He served it with an apology: they were out of the magnolia flower, but he could offer her a 'margarita' (a daisy).

Elderflower Margarita

1 ½ oz (45 ml) tequila
½ oz (15 ml) Cointreau
½ oz (15 ml) lemon or lime juice
1 oz (30 ml) elderflower cordial

Pour all the ingredients except elderflower cordial into a shaker filled with ice. Shake well and strain into a chilled cocktail glass. Add elderflower cordial and garnish with a lemon wedge.

The origin of the classic Margarita could have something to do with Marjorie King, an American show girl from the late 1930s who was allergic to all alcohol except tequila. Once when on holiday, she became tired of always having to drink shots and asked bartender Danny Herrera at Rancho Del Gloria Bar, Playa Rosarito, Mexico, to come up with a mixed drink for her. He named his new creation Margarita, Spanish for Marjorie.

Pineapple Margarita

1 oz (30 ml) tequila
1 oz (30 ml) Sourz Pineapple
½ oz (15 ml) lime juice

Pour all the ingredients into
a shaker filled with ice. Shake
well and strain into a chilled
cocktail glass.

*Another explanation for how the original version of the Margarita cocktail got its name concerns film
star Rita Hayworth. In the 1930s, as a teenager, she worked as a dancer at the Foreign Club in Tijuana.
That is where she is said to have inspired the bartender to create the new cocktail and name it after
her. Her real name, by the way, was Margarita Cansino.*

Japanese Margarita

1 ½ oz (45 ml) tequila,
  preferably Garcia Lemon
½ oz (15 ml) Midori melon
  liqueur
1 oz (30 ml) lime juice
1 lime wedge
Salt or sugar rim for garnish

Pour all the ingredients into
a shaker filled with ice. Shake
well and strain into a chilled
cocktail glass with a salt or
sugar rim.

Frosted rim: Pour salt or
sugar onto a saucer. Moisten
the rim of the glass with
the lime wedge and dip
the upturned glass into the
contents of the saucer.

*Midori, the Japanese word for 'green', is a bright green vanilla-flavoured melon liqueur manufactured by
the Japanese Suntory distillery. The liqueur had its big international breakthrough at the Studio 54 night
club in New York.*

Vanilla Peach Margarita

1 oz (30 ml) tequila
½ oz (15 ml) vanilla vodka
½ oz (15 ml) Cointreau
1 oz (30 ml) lime juice
2 oz (60 ml) peach purée
Salt or sugar rim for garnish

Pour all the ingredients
except peach purée into a
shaker filled with ice. Shake
well and strain into a chilled
Margarita glass with a salt or
sugar rim. Add peach purée
and stir gently.

Frosted rim: Pour salt or
sugar onto a saucer. Moisten
the rim of the glass with
the lime wedge and dip
the upturned glass into the
contents of the saucer.

*Vanilla comes from the Latin word for 'vagina' (because of the sheath-like shape of the capsules of the
vanilla flower, i.e. the vanilla pod). This symbolism may have been reason enough to inspire the German
18th century doctor Bezaar Zimmerman to claim that vanilla was an excellent aphrodisiac that could
cure impotence. A big breakthrough for vanilla in Europe followed …*

Strawberry Margarita

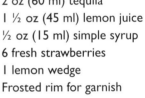

2 oz (60 ml) tequila
1 ½ oz (45 ml) lemon juice
½ oz (15 ml) simple syrup
6 fresh strawberries
1 lemon wedge
Frosted rim for garnish

Pour all the ingredients into a blender with crushed ice and mix them until 'half frozen' – stop before they turn into sorbet. Pour into a cocktail glass with a frosted rim.

Frosted rim: Pour salt or sugar onto a saucer. Moisten the rim of the glass with the lime wedge and dip the upturned glass into the contents of the saucer.

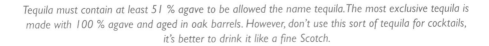

Tequila must contain at least 51 % agave to be allowed the name tequila. The most exclusive tequila is made with 100 % agave and aged in oak barrels. However, don't use this sort of tequila for cocktails, it's better to drink it like a fine Scotch.

Dirty Martini

2 oz (60 ml) gin
½ oz (15 ml) Martini Extra Dry
½ oz (15 ml) olive brine
Green olives for garnish

Pour all the ingredients into a
mixing glass with plenty of ice
cubes. Stir well until chilled.
Strain into a chilled cocktail
glass and garnish with olives.

*Olive seeds have been found around old Stone Age settlements, making the olive one of the oldest
vegetables known to man. In cocktails, green olives are normally used. They are in fact nothing other
than unripe black olives that are frequently stuffed with a piece of red pepper. As to this cocktail,
someone has spilled brine into their Dry Martini, to the delight of all olive lovers.*

Dry Martini

2 oz (60 ml) gin, e.g. Tanqueray
  or Bombay Sapphire
½ oz (15 ml) dry vermouth
Green olives for garnish

Pour gin and vermouth into a
mixing glass with plenty of ice
cubes. Stir well until chilled.
Strain into a chilled cocktail
glass and garnish with olives.

*TIP! Exchange gin for vodka and
get yourself a 'vodkatini' (which
should be shaken, not stirred). In
the film Casino Royal, James Bond
drinks a hybrid between the two,
which he names after his lady friend
in the film – Vesper. 'Because of the
bitter aftertaste?' she wonders. He
replies: 'Because after you've tasted
it…you won't drink anything else.'*

*A Dry Martini should indeed be dry. The smaller the amount of vermouth, the drier the Martini,
according to some. This is not entirely true. A fine, dry vermouth is necessary, otherwise you are left with
a glass of gin, not a cocktail. 1 part vermouth to 5 parts gin is not unusual, but bartenders' opinions
have varied over the years. Ask any bartender today and he will claim his recipe to be the right one …*

Appletini

1 oz (30 ml) vodka
1 oz (30 ml) sour apple liqueur
½ oz (15 ml) lemon juice

Pour all the ingredients except lemon juice into a shaker filled with ice. Shake well and strain into a chilled cocktail glass. Squirt some lemon juice on top and garnish with green apple.

TIP! *Fancy a more moderate Appletini? Replace half the amount of alcohol with apple juice.*

This is Dr Dorian's beloved cocktail from the TV-comedy Scrubs. A girl's drink, some laugh. He defends his choice and claims it to be a 'straight guy's' cocktail. However, he is careful with the alcohol and orders it with the words: 'Easy on the tini' …

Chilli Martini

2 oz (60 ml) lemon grass vodka
½ oz (15 ml) simple syrup
Red chilli pepper
Lemon grass as a flavouring

Remove the seeds from the chilli pepper and chop the fruit finely. Put the chopped chilli with the other ingredients in a shaker filled with ice. Shake well and strain into a chilled cocktail glass. Garnish with fresh chilli pepper.

TIP! *As lemon grass vodka may be hard to find in the shops, make your own by beating a stick of lemon grass with a hammer and then putting it in a bottle of vodka. Let it infuse for about a week.*

Lemon grass has a mild citrus flavour and is a common herb in Asian cuisine. Modern research has started to take an interest in one of its active substances, which has the ability to destroy cancer cells while leaving healthy cells unharmed. A fact that hardly makes this Martini a health bomb …

Grapetini

2 oz (60 ml) vanilla vodka
2 oz (60 ml) Tropicana Ruby
  Breakfast
Egg white

Pour all the ingredients into
a shaker filled with ice. Shake
well and strain into a chilled
cocktail glass.

*This was somebody's favourite breakfast juice, which suddenly
got to play the leading role in its very own cocktail.*

French Martini

1 oz (30 ml) vodka
1 oz (30 ml) Crème de Mûre
½ oz (15 ml) pineapple juice
½ oz (15 ml) lemon juice
½ oz (15 ml) simple syrup

Pour all the ingredients into a shaker filled with ice. Shake well and strain into a chilled cocktail glass.

TIP! *Add some Cointreau for an exciting flavour sensation.*

No gin, no vermouth, no olive. On the other hand: juice, sugar and liqueur. Dry Martini lovers don't know what the heck is going on. Neither do we. Maybe the French know? All the same, it's delicious!

Strawberry Martini

2 oz (60 ml) gin
1 oz (15 ml) dry vermouth
1 oz (15 ml) strawberry cordial

Pour all the ingredients into a mixing glass with plenty of ice cubes. Stir well until chilled. Strain into a chilled cocktail glass and garnish with fresh strawberries.

Winston Churchill believed that the best way of mixing a Dry Martini was to pour a glass of gin and then throw a glance at the vermouth bottle – only then would it be it dry enough. We wonder what Churchill would have said about this 'distortion' of one of the world's most famous cocktails …

Pomegranatini

1 ½ oz (45 ml) vodka
½ oz (15 ml) pomegranate
  liqueur
1 oz (30 ml) pomegranate juice
½ oz (15 ml) cranberry juice
½ oz (15 ml) lime juice

Pour all the ingredients into
a shaker filled with ice. Shake
well and strain into a chilled
cocktail glass.

The pomegranate appears frequently in the Bible,
where it is mostly mentioned in a romantic or poetic context.

Sweet Martini

2 oz (30 ml) gin
½ oz (15 ml) red vermouth
Cherries for garnish

Pour all the ingredients into
a mixing glass with plenty
of ice cubes. Stir well until
chilled. Strain into a chilled
cocktail glass and garnish with
cherries.

*Bernard 'Monty' Montgomery, legendary British commander during WW2, preferred his Dry Martini
with the proportions 9 to 1 – the same proportion in strength he desired between his own soldiers and
the enemy. He would probably not have appreciated this sweet version …*

Coriander & Chilli

2 oz (60 ml) Havana Club
 Añejo Reserva
1 oz (30 ml) simple syrup
1 oz lemon juice
1 piece chilli pepper
1 piece lemongrass
1 bunch coriander

Muddle all the ingredients
except the rum in a shaker.
Fill up with crushed ice and
rum. Give it a good shake.
Strain into a cocktail glass.
Garnish with herbs and spices.

*Coriander is one of our oldest herbs, mentioned as early as 1550 BC. In China, it was common belief
that the herb gave eternal life. Be that as it may, it is certainly rich in antioxidants and has been used in
medicine because of its antibacterial properties.*

My Funny Valentine

1 oz (30 ml) vanilla vodka
1 oz (30 ml) raspberry liqueur
Sparkling white wine
Frozen raspberries for garnish

Pour the liqueur and the
vodka into a champagne
glass and stir. Fill up with
ice-cold sparkling wine. Let a
few frozen raspberries bob
romantically in the drink
while it is being chilled.

*In a recent study, men and women were asked to name their favourite Valentine's Day activity. A nice
dinner, was the most common answer. This is the perfect start to a romantic evening for two.*

Absolut Green Wedding

1 ½ oz (45 ml) Absolut Vodka
½ oz (15 ml) melon liqueur
Champagne
1 dash lime cordial
Maraschino cherries for garnish

Pour the liqueur and the
vodka into a champagne glass
and stir. Fill up with ice-cold
champagne or sparkling
wine. Top with a dash of
lime cordial and garnish with
maraschino cherries.

Anything can be organic these days — even the most important day of your life!
Visit www.greenishwedding.com to get 101 tips for your own green wedding.
A green aperitif is a must on such an occasion!

Bellini

1 oz (30 ml) peach puree
Dry sparkling wine
(The original is made with
  Italian Prosecco)

Pour the puree into a chilled
champagne glass. Fill up with
ice-cold sparkling wine and
stir gently.

TIP! *Peach puree may be hard to
come by, and if so, use peach juice
instead. If you can't find peach
juice, why not do like Mr Cipriani
himself and make your own puree
by blending fresh peaches...*

*This all-time classic was created at Harry's Bar in Venice in the 1940s where, until this day, Bellinis are
made with fresh, white peaches mixed and a touch of lemon while guests wait. The beautiful colour
reminded bartender Giuseppe Cipriani of the sunset in a painting by the Venetian 15th century painter
Giovanni Bellini and thus named his new drink after him.*

Blackberry Bellini

1 ½ oz (45 ml) blackberry
    puree
1 oz (30 ml) Crème de Mûre
Dry sparkling wine
Blackberries for garnish

Pour the liqueur and
the puree into a chilled
champagne glass. Fill up with
ice-cold sparkling wine. Stir
gently and garnish with fresh
blackberries on a skewer.

TIP! *You can make a delicious
Bellini with any type of puree.
Choose what happens to be in
season. Here is a version with
liqueur backup.*

*The original is traditionally served at all special occasions in Venice as well as all over Italy.
Bellini is the perfect aperitif at weddings and other celebrations. For kids, non-alcoholic cider
is used to fill up the glass.*

Kir Royale

1 ½ oz (45 ml) Crème de
  Cassis
Champagne

Pour the liqueur into a chilled
champagne glass. Fill up with
ice-cold champagne (or
sparkling wine).

TIP! *The original, Kir, is made by
replacing champagne with a dry,
white Burgundy wine.*

*Kir is named after Felix Kir, mayor of the French city of Dijon between 1945 and 1968. By marketing
the drink as Burgundy's official cocktail and always serving it at local official events, he managed
to save the grape as well as the wine from financial ruin. Royals are usually served Kir made with
champagne.*

Queen's Delight

2 oz (60 ml) gin
1–2 tbsp raspberry jam
Lemonade

Pour the gin into a chilled
champagne glass and fill
up with crushed ice. Add
raspberry jam and top up
with lemonade. Garnish with
fresh berries.

Gin was long considered a working classes drink. This was at a time when the nobility, regardless of nationality, spoke French to each other and drank cognac. Today, gin is consumed everywhere, even in royal palaces...

Rossini

1 ½ oz (45 ml) frozen
strawberries
½ oz (15 ml) lemon juice
½ oz (15 ml) simple syrup
Sparkling wine

Mix the frozen strawberries
in a blender until pureed. Add
lemon juice and simple syrup.
Pour about 1 ½ oz (45 ml) of
the puree into a champagne
glass. Fill up with ice-cold
champagne or sparkling wine.
Garnish with a raspberry on
the rim and serve immediately,
while the bubbles are fresh
and sparkling.

This is a romantic, rose-coloured treat for Valentine's Day! Or why not try a Bellini, another tasty Italian champagne cocktail.

Ritz Fizz

½ oz (15 ml) blue curaçao
½ oz (15 ml) amaretto
½ oz (15 ml) lemon juice
Champagne
Fresh blueberries for garnish

Pour the curaçao, amaretto
and lemon juice into a
chilled champagne glass. Fill
up with chilled champagne
and stir gently. Garnish with
blueberries.

*The Ritz Fizz was created as the Ritz-Carlton hotel chain's signature cocktail in 1934 upon the
repealing of the Prohibition. It was first concocted in the bar at the former Ritz-Carlton Hotel in Boston,
Massachusetts.*

Short Drinks

'Eating is a need for the stomach.
Drinking is a need for the soul.'

Claude Tiller

Short drinks are usually served in various sorts of low glasses without a stem. Unlike long drinks, they consist mainly of alcohol. Short drinks served in a glass without a stem – as opposed to short drinks in high-stemmed glasses (cocktails) – are often served with ice cubes ('on the rocks') or with crushed ice. The most common glass for these drinks is a tumbler, or a whisky glass – which is perhaps the term most people are familiar with. For the sake of simplicity, we have chosen to write 'tumbler' in the recipes as a generic term for all these glasses, with a few exceptions. Read more about glass types in the Glassware chapter at the beginning of the book.

When preparing any short drink, the contents are chilled using one of two methods – shaking or stirring with ice. The recipes will tell you which method to use.

A pre-dinner aperitif is more often than not a short drink. You drink it quickly, and it traditionally consists of ingredients that are said to stimulate the appetite –whisky, vermouth or Campari. As a non-alcoholic alternative, try serving fruit and vegetable juices in cocktail glasses. After dinner, a 'digestif' is often served. It usually has a higher alcoholic content than an aperitif in order to aid digestion. Or try a distillate of fruit or berries, but that's another story.

Americano

1 oz (30 ml) Campari
1 oz (30 ml) red vermouth
Orange wedge and lemon
 peel for garnish

Pour all the ingredients into
a tumbler filled with ice and
stir. If desired, top with some
soda. Garnish with an orange
wedge and a lemon twist.

TIP! *This cocktail is excellent as
a long drink too – serve it in a
highball glass and fill up with soda.*

*This bittersweet mix of grape distillates is a popular Italian classic, created around 1860 by Gaspare
Campari in his bar, the Campari Bar. He named the drink 'Milan-Turin' after his own hometown and
the city where Cinzano vermouth is produced respectively. During the American Prohibition, most bar
guests were American, and the drink was renamed in their honour.*

Black Russian

1 oz (30 ml) vodka
1 oz (30 ml) Kahlúa

Pour the ingredients into a
tumbler filled with ice and stir.

TIP! *The original recipe contained*
Tia Maria liqueur, but the
ambassadress probably doesn't
mind that most bartenders today
use Kahlúa instead.

Barman Gustave Tops is said to have created the world's most famous 'on the rocks' (with the
exception of whisky on the rocks and a few other classics) at the Hotel Metropole in Brussels around
1950. Harry Truman's envoy to Luxemburg, ambassador Mrs. Pearl Mesta, is said to have particularly
appreciated the drink.

Raspberry Black Russian

1 oz (30 ml) raspberry vodka
1 oz (30 ml) Kahlúa
Fresh raspberries for garnish

Pour the ingredients into a
tumbler filled with ice and stir.
Garnish with raspberries.

*A raspberry-flavoured half-sister of the Black Russian. See also White Russian, which is made with
cream. Sweet and fruity, perfect for summer dinners on the balcony!*

Ferrari

1 ½ oz (45 ml) dry vermouth
½ oz (15 ml) amaretto
2 dashes Angostura Bitter
Lemon peel

Pour all the ingredients into a
mixing glass with plenty of ice
cubes. Stir well until chilled.
Strain into a chilled tumbler.
Squeeze some oil out of
the lemon peel as a flavour-
enhancer, and drop the peel
into the glass as a garnish.

TIP! *Make sure that the white,
bitter pith does not end up in the
drink, it could completely ruin the
cocktail. Use a lemon zester to
make the peel nice and thin.*

*Angostura is the bitter aromatic bark of certain trees that grow around the Orinoco River in Venezuela.
Angostura bitters can also be used in salad dressings.*

Bramble

1 ½ oz (45 ml) gin
½ oz (15 ml) Crème de Mûre
1 oz (30 ml) lemon juice
½ oz (15 ml) simple syrup

Pour the gin, lemon juice
and simple syrup into a
tumbler filled with ice and stir.
Carefully drizzle the liqueur
over the ice cubes. Garnish
with fresh blackberries.

Bramble is a family of plants that also includes blackberry and raspberry.
Try a Bramble made with raspberry liqueur for variation.

Brave Bull

1 ½ oz (45 ml) tequila
½ oz (15 ml) Kahlúa

Pour the ingredients into a
tumbler filled with ice and stir.

Two of Mexico's prides sharing one glass in perfect harmony.

Chapala

1 ½ oz (45 ml) tequila
½ oz (15 ml) triple sec
1 ½ oz (45 ml) orange juice
½ oz (15 ml) lemon juice
½ oz (15 ml) grenadine
Chilli pepper for garnish

Pour all the ingredients into a shaker filled with ice. Shake well and strain into a chilled tumbler or a small highball glass. Make a small incision in a chilli pepper and hang it on the rim.

Triple sec is a citrus-flavoured liqueur. It can in most cases be replaced with Cointreau.
Triple Sec was created in 1834. The original is still made from sundried orange peel and distilled in
100-year-old copper stills in Haiti.

El Niño

1 oz (30 ml) Pisco
1 oz (30 ml) Limoncello
8 grapes
1 oz (30 ml) raspberry puree
1 oz (30 ml) blackberry puree
1 oz (30 ml) apple juice
½ oz (15 ml) lemon juice
½ oz (15 ml) simple syrup

Muddle 4 of the grapes in a shaker. Fill up with ice cubes, add all the other ingredients and shake well. Strain into a tumbler filled with ice and garnish with grapes.

TIP! *In Chile and Peru, where the grape spirit is produced, Pisco Sour is a local favourite. It is easy to mix – equal parts Pisco and lemon juice. Simply add ice, egg white and simple syrup.*

This short drink is named after the unpredictable weather phenomenon that is a constant cause of flooding along South America's west coast. The Peruvian coastal population have named the phenomenon El Niño, which in Spanish means 'the boy' (baby Jesus), as the phenomenon usually occurs around Christmas.

Elite

1 ½ oz (45 ml) bourbon
½ oz (15 ml) raspberry
   liqueur
2 dashes Licor 43
1 oz (30 ml) raspberry puree
½ oz (15 ml) simple syrup
1 oz (30 ml) lemon juice

Pour the ingredients into a
tumbler and stir. Fill up with
crushed ice.

*Licor 43, also known as 'Cuarenta Y Tres', is a Spanish, bright yellow liqueur made from citrus fruits and
flavoured with vanilla and many other aromatic plants. The liqueur contains 43 different ingredients
(hence the name).*

Kamikaze

1 ½ oz (45 ml) vodka
½ oz (15 ml) Cointreau
1 oz (30 ml) lemon juice
Lemon grass for garnish

Pour all the ingredients into
a shaker filled with ice. Shake
well and strain into a chilled
tumbler. Place some lemon
grass or lime peel in the glass
as a garnish.

*When attempting to attack Japan in 1281, the Mongol fleet was held back by a powerful storm. The
Japanese named the storm 'Kamikaze', which means 'divine wind'. Several hundred years later the
name was used again, this time for the Japanese suicide pilots who voluntarily crashed their aircrafts
against American ships. In translation, the name of this short drink comes to mean 'a divine suicide
drink', perhaps because you'll want a few sips more than you can handle...*

French Connection

1 oz (30 ml) brandy
1 oz (30 ml) amaretto
Soda water to taste

Pour all the ingredients in a tumbler filled with ice. Top with soda and stir.

Brandy is a distilled spirit made from grapes. Cognac, the best known type, originates from the Cognac region in south-western France. As the distillate was capable of surviving long journeys without affecting the flavour, it quickly spread across Europe. It became particularly popular in Holland during the 80-year-long war against Spain, when people were unwilling to drink Spanish wine.

Gin By You

1 ½ oz (45 ml) gin
½ oz (15 ml) Absolut Kurant
½ oz (15 ml) lemon juice

Pour all the ingredients into a mixing glass with plenty of ice cubes. Stir well until chilled. Strain into a chilled tumbler and garnish with red berries.

This is a version of the slightly better known cocktail Gin By Me, which includes lime juice instead of lemon juice.

Gimlet

2 oz (60 ml) gin
1 oz (30 ml) lime cordial

Pour all the ingredients into a tumbler and stir. Fill up with crushed ice. Garnish with a flower, or, if you have a sense of humour and want to honour history – a corkscrew!

A law was passed in 1867 for the entire British Royal Navy in order to prevent outbreaks of scurvy on board – all ships had to carry supplies of lime juice for the sailors. The sailors, who preferred gin, compromised and poured the lime juice into their glasses of gin. The new short drink was named after the corkscrew-like tool that was used to open the barrels of lime juice.

Godmother

1 ½ oz (45 ml) vodka
½ oz (15 ml) amaretto

Pour all the ingredients into a
tumbler filled with ice and stir.

Sleeping Beauty had one wicked godmother and eleven good ones.
Who could this be?

Godfather

1 ½ oz (45 ml) whisky
½ oz (15 ml) amaretto

Pour all the ingredients in a
tumbler filled with ice and stir.

A real mafioso or a nice godfather at the christening?
Try it, and decide for yourself!

Hemingway Special

2 oz (60 ml) light rum
1 oz (30 ml) grapefruit juice
1 dash red maraschino liqueur
½ oz (15 ml) lemon juice

Pour all the ingredients into
a shaker filled with ice. Shake
and strain into a tumbler. Fill
up the glass with crushed ice.

TIP! *In many recipes, you'll find
lime rather than lemon juice. Try
both versions and decide on your
favourite!*

*Since Hemingway was diabetic, his Cuban bartender 'Constante' Ribalaigua at La Floridita used to mix
this very special Daiquiri for him, which contained no sugar, but grapefruit juice instead. Legend has it
that Hemingway was partly responsible for the recipe: 'Forget about the sugar and double the amount
of booze!' is a quote attributed to him. Both the drink and the author himself are sometimes referred to
as 'Papa Double'.*

Nacional de Cuba

1 ½ oz (45 ml) aged rum
½ oz (15 ml) apricot brandy
½ oz (15 ml) lime juice
1 oz (30 ml) pineapple juice
Fresh pineapple

Muddle a chunk of pineapple in a tumbler. Fill up with crushed ice to the brim. Add all the other ingredients and stir. Serve with a straw and a cocktail stick.

'National de Cuba' generally refers to a major hotel in Havana. The town's ballet academy bears the same name. In this case, the national drink of Cuba has been honoured with the name. A classic Nacional is mixed with Cuban rum, usually one of the light types. However, matured rum is sometimes used, often in combination with pineapple instead of simple syrup, as in the above recipe.

Juicy Fruit

1 ½ oz (45 ml) Absolut Vanilia
½ oz (15 ml) butterscotch
  schnapps
1 oz (30 ml) passion fruit syrup
3 lemon wedges
5 mint leaves

Muddle lemon wedges and
mint leaves gently in a highball
glass. Fill up with crushed ice,
add the rest of the ingredients
and stir. Garnish with papaya
or passion fruit.

*Butterscotch schnapps is a popular liqueur with a lovely caramel flavour. 'Butterscotch' is quite a
peculiar word and the meaning of the word 'scotch' is thought to be 'to cut or score', as the popular
confectionery must be cut into pieces, or 'scotched', before hardening.*

Mint Julep

2 oz (60 ml) bourbon
8–10 mint leaves
½ oz (15 ml) simple syrup

Muddle the mint leaves and simple syrup gently in a tumbler. Fill up with crushed ice, add bourbon and stir. Garnish with mint leaves.

One of the oldest drinks in American history, it used to be drunk for breakfast (!) by peasants in the south who needed something to prepare themselves for a long and strenuous day working in the fields. The cocktail is highly popular today, for example at The Kentucky Derby. The word 'julep' comes from the Arabic word 'julab', which means 'made of rose petals'.

Misty Bitch

1 oz (30 ml) vodka
1 oz (30 ml) Campari
½ oz (15 ml) lime juice
½ oz (15 ml) pink grapefruit
  juice

Pour all the ingredients into
a shaker filled with ice. Shake
well and strain into an ice-
filled tumbler.

TIP! *If you want the Campari to
form a layer at the bottom of the
glass as a colour effect, make layers
of the rest of the ingredients on top.
(Read more about layering in the
beginning of the book.)*

'A real bitch swallows her bitterness instead of letting it speak.'
This may have been what the creator of this Campari short drink was thinking...

Negroni

¾ oz (20 ml) gin
¾ oz (20 ml) Campari
¾ oz (20 ml) red vermouth
Lemon wedge for garnish

Pour all the ingredients into a tumbler filled with ice and stir. Put a lemon wedge in the glass as garnish.

TIP! *Adding a splash of soda in the drink is optional, which is why it is sometimes served in a shot glass on the side. If you want more soda, choose a bigger glass.*

Count Camillo Negroni was a frequent guest at the Casoni Bar in Florence, but he did not really like the taste of the popular short drink Americano. He persistently asked the bartender to spike it with gin. The bartender named the result after his fastidious – but creative – guest.

Old Fashioned

2 oz (60 ml) bourbon
1 sugar cube
2 dashes Angostura Bitter
1 splash soda water
Maraschino cherries
Orange slice

Place a sugar cube in an Old Fashioned glass (if you have one, otherwise a normal tumbler will do) and add the Angostura Bitter. Wait until the sugar cube has absorbed the bitters. Add a splash of soda and muddle until dissolved. Fill the glass with ice cubes and add the bourbon. Garnish with an orange slice, a lemon twist and a maraschino cherry.

TIP! *Spelling whisk(e)y can be tricky. When do we use the 'e'? As a rule, American and Irish prefer 'whiskey' and the Scots, Canadians and the rest of the world's single malt makers prefer 'whisky'.*

'Make it another Old Fashioned,' Cole Porter wrote in one of his songs. This is the classic and simple drink which had a glass named after it. It is often served with a spoon for mashing the cherry and orange slice if desired.

Rusty Nail

1 ½ oz (45 ml) Scotch
½ oz (15 ml) Drambuie

Pour the Scotch and
Drambuie in a tumbler filled
with ice and stir.

Two Scotsmen hitting it off in one glass!

Winter Apple

1 oz (30 ml) vodka
1 oz (30 ml) calvados
½ oz (15 ml) lemon juice
½ oz (15 ml) simple syrup
Cinnamon stick and diced
  apple for garnish

Pour the syrup and lemon
juice into a tumbler. Fill up
with crushed ice and diced
apple in layers. Add the vodka
and the liqueur and stir gently.
Garnish with a cinnamon
stick.

TIP! *Cocktails served with crushed
ice may need a straw if you don't
fancy ice crunching between your
teeth …*

*France is famous for its wines, but in the Calvados region, located in the north-eastern corner of the
country, it is too cold to grow grapes. Instead, they grow apples for making cider. This was where the
apple brandy with the same name first saw the light of day.*

Blueberry Sour

1 ½ oz (45 ml) Absolut Vanilia
½ oz (15 ml) blueberry liqueur
1 oz (30 ml) lemon juice
½ oz (15 ml) simple syrup
Blueberries for garnish

Pour all the ingredients into a shaker filled with ice. Shake well and strain into an ice-filled tumbler. Garnish with blueberries on a skewer.

TIP! *If you fancy a bit of froth, pour some egg white into the shaker.*

Have you ever wondered why vanilla is so popular all over the world?
It is because it is a flavour found in is in fact found in mother's milk.

Brandy Sour

2 oz (60 ml) brandy
1 oz (30 ml) lemon juice
½ oz (15 ml) simple syrup
Egg white

Pour all ingredients into a shaker filled with ice. Shake well and strain into an ice-filled tumbler. The egg white gives a nice, long-lasting froth, which is one of the characteristics of sour drinks, but not an absolute necessity.

A classic sour is usually shaken with egg white to create the visual effect of a frothy surface. But it contributes nothing to the flavour, and many who are not fond of the idea of drinking raw eggs simply skip it. Well-stocked shops sell artificial cocktail froth.

Gin Sour

2 oz (60 ml) gin
1 oz (30 ml) lemon juice
½ oz (15 ml) simple syrup
Egg white

Pour all the ingredients
into a shaker filled with ice.
Shake well and strain into
an ice-filled tumbler. The egg
white gives a nice, long-lasting
froth which is one of the
characteristics of sour drinks,
but not an absolute necessity.

TIP! *There is an infinite variety of
sour drinks. Take your favourite spirit
and follow the instructions. Popular
versions are Whisky Sour and Vodka
Sour. If you don't fancy raw eggs
in your drink, replace them with
artificial cocktail froth.*

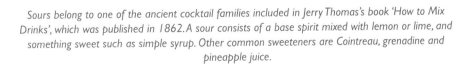

*Sours belong to one of the ancient cocktail families included in Jerry Thomas's book 'How to Mix
Drinks', which was published in 1862. A sour consists of a base spirit mixed with lemon or lime, and
something sweet such as simple syrup. Other common sweeteners are Cointreau, grenadine and
pineapple juice.*

Whisky Sour

2 oz (60 ml) whisky
1 oz (30 ml) lemon juice
½ oz (15 ml) simple syrup

Pour all the ingredients into a shaker filled with ice. Shake well and strain into a chilled, ice-filled tumbler.

A classic Whisk(e)y Sour is based on bourbon. Other types of whisky, Scotch for example, which adds a slightly smoky flavour, are fine too. If you don't like the strong stuff, try a Liqueur Sour. Shake 2 oz of your favourite liqueur with 1 oz of lemon juice and you have an Amaretto Sour, Tia Maria Sour or a Grand Marnier Sour.

New York Sour

2 oz (60 ml) bourbon
1 oz (30 ml) orange juice
¾ oz (20 ml) lemon juice
½ oz (15 ml) simple syrup
Egg white
½ oz (15 ml) red wine

Pour all the ingredients except the red wine into a shaker filled with ice. Shake well and strain into a chilled, ice-filled tumbler. Float red wine on top.

New York Sour exists in different versions. All recipes are based on a Whisky Sour topped with red wine or port. The rest is up to the bartender.

Caipirinha

2 oz (60 ml) Cachaça
2 lime wedges
2 tsp granulated sugar

Muddle the lime wedges and sugar in a tumbler. Fill up with crushed ice, add Cachaça and stir. Serve with a straw and a cocktail stick.

TIP! *To mix a Caipirissima, replace the Cachaça with light rum. Replace it with sake and you get a Caipisake!*

Caipirinha literally means 'peasant drink'. It is a Brazilian short drink made with the national spirit, Cachaça. The difference between rum and Cachaça is that rum is usually made from molasses (a mineral-rich by-product of sugar) while Cachaça is made from freshly squeezed sugar cane juice.

Ginger Kumquat Caipirinha

2 oz (60 ml) Cachaça
4 kumquats, sliced
1 tsp fresh ginger, chopped
½ oz (15 ml) simple syrup
Ginger for garnish

Muddle the ginger, kumquats and simple syrup in a tumbler. Fill up with crushed ice, add Cachaça and stir. Garnish with a piece of fresh ginger and serve with a straw and a cocktail stick.

TIP! *Kumquats should be eaten whole – the sweetness is in the peel!*

The complex combination of fresh ginger, kumquats and Cachaça is an exciting taste experience you should try at least once in a lifetime. Kumquats are small citrus fruits that reached Europe in the mid-1800s from China and Japan. Sliced kumquat is often used to flavour green tea and salads as well as chocolate desserts. Pickled kumquats are delicious in meat dishes and kumquat marmalade is excellent.

Blackcurrant Caipirinha

1 ½ oz (45 ml) Cachaça
½ oz (15 ml) Crème de Cassis
2 lime wedges
½ oz (15 ml) simple syrup
Blackcurrants for garnish

Muddle the lime and syrup
in a glass. Fill up with
crushed ice, add Cachaça and
liqueur and stir. Add some
blackcurrants on top. Serve
with a straw and a cocktail
stick.

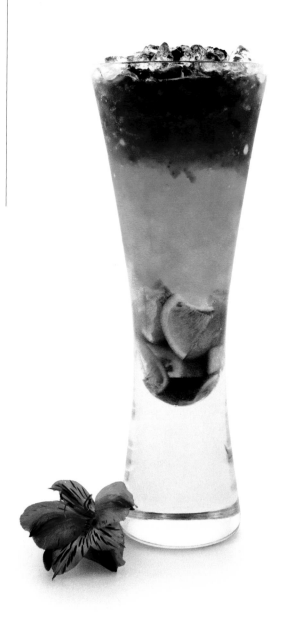

Cachaça is a type of light rum made entirely from sugar cane juice and distilled in single columns. In its more concentrated form, it's called 'rhum agricole'. There are many different brands of Cachaça, which is produced exclusively in Brazil. However, the rhum agricole method is used with other types of rum too, including rum made in Haiti or Martinique.

Tropical Caipirinha

1 ½ oz (45 ml) Cachaça
½ oz (15 ml) amaretto
2 lime wedges
1 oz (30 ml) pineapple juice
1 oz (30 ml) guava juice

Muddle the lime in a tumbler. Fill up with crushed ice, add Cachaça and amaretto and stir. Garnish in a tropical fashion and serve with a straw and a cocktail stick.

Cachaça is made from freshly squeezed sugar cane juice instead of molasses, which preserves the sweetness. Cachaça must contain 100% sugar cane distillate and be produced in Brazil. Caipirinha is the most famous Cachaça cocktail. It exists in many fruity variations, just like the Cuban rum cocktail Mojito.

Caipiroska

2 oz (60 ml) vodka
2 lime wedges
3 tsp granulated sugar

Muddle the lime and sugar in a tumbler. Fill up with crushed ice, add vodka and stir. Serve with a straw and a cocktail stick.

A Caipiroska is a Caipirinha with vodka instead of rum. Its popularity has increased rapidly during recent years along with the introduction of more international vodka brands in Brazil.

Sweetheart Caipiroska

2 oz (60 ml) Absolut Raspberri
½ oz (15 ml) lemon juice
½ oz (15 ml) grenadine
Strawberries for garnish

Pour the lemon juice into a tumbler. Fill up with crushed ice and sliced strawberries. Add the vodka and stir. Add the grenadine in drops and stir. Serve with a straw and a cocktail stick.

In ancient Rome, the goddess Juno was often depicted holding a pomegranate as a symbol of marriage.
So this is the perfect drink to offer your sweetheart. Grenadine is based on pomegranate juice, and has
a very concentrated sweetness, just like the one you love...

Nordic Lingonberry Caipiroska

2 oz (60 ml) lingonberry vodka
½ oz (15 ml) lemon juice
½ oz (15 ml) simple syrup
1 dash grenadine
Fresh lingonberries for garnish

Pour the lemon juice and simple syrup into a tumbler. Fill up the glass with crushed ice mixed with fresh lingonberries. Add vodka and stir. Top with a dash of grenadine. Serve with a straw and a cocktail stick.

TIP! *Are lingonberries hard to come by? Use cranberries instead!*

A Caipiroska, made with vodka instead of Cachaça rum, is a sibling of the Caipirinha. In Brazil, the drink often goes by the name of Caipivodka. Lingonberries grow wild in Northern Europe, but you may know it by a different name: cowberry, foxberry, quailberry, mountain cranberry, red whortleberry, lowbush cranberry, mountain bilberry, partridgeberry or simply redberry.

Nordic Blueberry Caipiroska

2 oz (60 ml) blueberry vodka
½ oz (15 ml) lemon juice
½ oz (15 ml) simple syrup
1 dash blue curaçao
Fresh blueberries for garnish

Pour the lemon juice
and simple syrup into a
tumbler. Fill up the glass
with crushed ice mixed with
fresh blueberries. Add vodka
and stir. Top with a dash of
curaçao. Serve with a straw
and a cocktail stick.

*You might mistake the sweet blueberry for its relative, the bilberry, which is edible, but has a much
more watery, bland flavour. Bilberries are oval and their leaves a darker shade of green, but a bilberry
or two could still end up at the bottom of your basket and water down your blueberry pie...*

Frozen Cocktails

'Alcohol may be man's worst enemy,
but the bible says love your enemy.'

Frank Sinatra

Frozen cocktails are ice-cream for grownups. Forget all you know about ice and mixing techniques, the cocktails in this group are not served with ice, they are ice. The ingredients are mixed with ice with the help of an electric blender and served in more or less liquid form, not unlike sorbet. The names of these drinks often contain the word 'frozen', especially if a non-frozen cocktail of the same type exists. The popular Frozen Strawberry Daiquiri is one example.

Frozen cocktails are wonderfully refreshing on hot summer days, and are also excellent after a heavy meal. A frozen cocktail can be eaten with a spoon, but if you prefer to drink it, simply use less ice. The degree of 'frozenness' is a matter of personal preference. Pour the ice into the blender a little at a time until you reach the appropriate thickness. If possible, use crushed ice rather than ice cubes to spare the blades.

Some creamy drinks are lovely when served extra cold, but not quite like ice-cream. These can be blended with a little ice until 'half-frozen'. Make sure that any toddlers around don't think that you have made them a milkshake...

Frozen Mojito

2 oz (60 ml) light rum
1 oz (30 ml) lime juice
½ oz (15 ml) simple syrup
6–10 mint leaves

Pour all the ingredients into a blender. Blend briefly at high speed until smooth. Start with a small amount of crushed ice and add more until you get the desired thickness. Serve in a cocktail glass.

Mojito was one of Ernest Hemingway's favourite drinks during his time in Cuba. He used to enjoy them at La Bodeguita del Medio in Havana. The author is part of the reason why this Cuban drink has become so successful worldwide. This is the frozen form, which is almost as famous as the original. (The more mint leaves, the greener the Mojito.)

Frozen Daiquiri

2 oz (60 ml) light rum
1 oz (30 ml) lime juice
½ oz (15 ml) simple syrup
Crushed ice

Pour all the ingredients into a
blender. Blend briefly at high
speed until smooth. Start with
a small amount of crushed
ice and add more until you
achieve the desired thickness.
Serve in a margarita glass.

TIP! *Try adding a scoop of vanilla
ice-cream for variation.*

*Engineer Jennings, manager of the Daiquiri mine in eastern Cuba, once wanted to serve his visiting
colleague Pagliuchi a drink. Unfortunately, the storage room contained only rum, a little sugar and a few
lemons. They blended everything with ice and drank it. – 'What's the name of this drink then?' asked
Pagliuchi. 'Probably Rum Sour,' said Jennings. Pagliuchi replied that it was way too good to have such a
simple name: 'Let's call it Daiquiri!' These days Daiquiris are often mixed with lime.*

Frozen Blackberry Daiquiri

1 ½ oz (45 ml) golden rum
½ oz (15 ml) Crème de Mûre
5 blackberries
1 oz (30 ml) lemon juice
½ oz (15 ml) honey
Crushed ice

Pour all the ingredients into a blender. Blend briefly at high speed until smooth. Start with a small amount of crushed ice and add more until you achieve the desired thickness. Serve in a margarita glass and garnish with lemon balm.

Frozen Daiquiri is a common Daiquiri variation. Besides rum, lime juice and simple syrup, it contains crushed ice and fruit or berries. For a more intense flavour, add a matching liqueur, as we have done here.

Frozen Blueberry Daiquiri

1 oz (30 ml) light rum
1 oz (30 ml) blueberry liqueur
2 oz (60 ml) blueberries
1 oz (30 ml) lime juice
½ oz (15 ml) simple syrup
Crushed ice

Pour all the ingredients into a blender. Blend briefly at high speed until smooth. Start with a small amount of crushed ice and add more until you achieve the desired thickness. Serve in a margarita glass and garnish with lemon balm.

TIP! *You can also try using home-made or a commercial brand of blueberry puree.*

Nordic forest fruits meet the national spirit of Cuba and the summer is saved.

Frozen Banana Daiquiri

2 oz (60 ml) light rum
½ banana
1 oz (30 ml) lime or lemon
  juice
½ oz (15 ml) simple syrup
Crushed ice

Pour all the ingredients into a
blender. Blend briefly at high
speed until smooth. Start with
a small amount of crushed
ice and add more until you
achieve the desired thickness.
Serve in a margarita glass.

*Daiquiri comes in a million versions over and above the original cocktail of rum, citrus and sugar.
Legendary bartender Constante made the Floridita restaurant famous with his own original version
made with maraschino liqueur and crushed ice. For Mr. Hemingway he added grapefruit juice instead
of sugar. Until this day, tourists and Cubans go on pilgrimages to the Floridita bar, where Daiquiris are
said to taste better than anywhere else in the world.*

Frozen Strawberry Daiquiri

2 oz (60 ml) light rum
4–6 strawberries
1 oz (30 ml) lime juice
½ oz (15 ml) simple syrup
Crushed ice

Pour all the ingredients into
a blender. Blend briefly at
high speed until smooth.
Start with a small amount of
crushed ice and add more
until you achieve the desired
thickness. Serve in a margarita
glass and garnish with fresh
strawberries.

*Almost as well-known as the original, frozen strawberry Daiquiri is simply a must in the summer.
It's bound to seduce just about anyone...*

Frozen Mango Daiquiri

2 oz (60 ml) light rum
1 ½ oz (45 ml) mango puree
1 oz (30 ml) lime juice
½ oz (15 ml) simple syrup
Crushed ice

Pour all the ingredients into a blender. Blend briefly at high speed until smooth. Start with a small amount of crushed ice and add more until you achieve the desired thickness. Serve in a margarita glass and garnish with mango slices.

Spirits can be made from cane or beet sugar, although beets are not accepted as a raw material for rum.

Frozen Peach Daiquiri

2 oz (60 ml) light rum
1 ½ oz (45 ml) peach puree
1 oz (30 ml) lime juice
½ oz (15 ml) simple syrup
Crushed ice

Pour all the ingredients into a blender. Blend briefly at high speed until smooth. Start with a small amount of crushed ice and add more until you achieve the desired thickness. Serve in a margarita glass.

TIP! *For a more intense peach flavour, replace the simple syrup with peach juice.*

Christopher Columbus brought the first sugar canes from Asia to Cuba in the 15th century, which is good for us, because it's impossible to produce rum without sugar.

Frozen Raspberry Daiquiri

2 oz (60 ml) Bacardi Razz
8–10 raspberries
1 oz (30 ml) lime juice
½ oz (15 ml) simple syrup
Crushed ice

Pour all the ingredients into a blender. Blend briefly at high speed until smooth. Start with a small amount of crushed ice and add more until you achieve the desired thickness. Serve in a margarita glass and garnish with fresh raspberries.

The trick of mixing a perfect original Daiquiri is to squeeze the lime gently to avoid the bitter juice from the peel. Blend the drink for a few seconds only, no longer. If you're not very experienced, you can always mix a flavoured Daiquiri instead, like the next one, which is made with raspberries. You can't go wrong, and it's incredibly tasty!

Frozen Strawberry Margarita

1 ½ oz (45 ml) tequila
½ oz (15 ml) Cointreau
½ oz (15 ml) lemon juice
½ oz (15 ml) simple syrup
½ oz (15 ml) strawberry syrup
5–6 fresh strawberries
Crushed ice

Pour all the ingredients into a blender. Blend briefly at high speed until smooth. Start with a small amount of crushed ice and add more until you achieve the desired thickness. Serve in a margarita glass.

TIP! *If desired, replace the fresh strawberries with 2 oz (60 ml) strawberry puree.*

Tequila, the proud national spirit of Mexico, is made from the agave plant. The agave is a spiky, cactus-like lily with thick blue-green leaves. It has been used as a kind of 'barbed wire' on walls to scare away intruders.

Frozen Peach Margarita

1 ½ oz (45 ml) tequila
½ oz (15 ml) Cointreau
½ oz (15 ml) lime juice
½ tinned peach
Peach for garnish
Crushed ice

Pour all the ingredients into a blender. Blend briefly at high speed until smooth. Start with a small amount of crushed ice and add more until you achieve the desired thickness. Serve in a margarita glass and garnish with a peach slice.

TIP! *Add the ice a little at a time and stop when you have added enough. The 'frozenness' of a frozen Margarita is optional.*

Instead of using tinned peaches, feel free to experiment with peach puree or fresh peaches, but make sure they are very ripe.

Frozen Chi Chi

2 oz (60 ml) vodka
1 oz (30 ml) thick coconut
  cream
1 ½ oz (45 ml) pineapple juice
Crushed ice

Pour all the ingredients into a
blender. Blend briefly at high
speed until smooth. Start with
a small amount of crushed
ice and add more until you
achieve the desired thickness.
Pour into a glass of your
choice and garnish with a
tropical touch.

TIP! *If you are not a fan of
coconut cream, try coconut liqueur
or coconut syrup instead. Add half a
banana for the right thickness.*

*Blue Hawaii made with curaçao and Chi Chi made
with vodka are both Piña Colada variations.*

Frozen Pomegranate Chi Chi

2 oz (60 ml) vodka
1 oz (30 ml) thick coconut
cream
1 ½ oz (45 ml) pomegranate
juice
Crushed ice

Pour all the ingredients into a
blender. Blend briefly at high
speed until smooth. Start with
a small amount of crushed
ice and add more until you
achieve the desired thickness.
Pour into a glass of your
choice and garnish with green
leaves.

*In ancient Greece, the pomegranate was the attribute of goddesses including Persephone, Aphrodite
and Athena. Since pomegranates contain a multitude of seeds, pomegranate trees were perceived from
early on as fertility symbols. They were planted on the graves of heroes to ensure that their offspring
would be numerous.*

Raspberry Kiss

1 oz (30 ml) white crème de cacao
1 oz (30 ml) raspberry liqueur
1 oz (30 ml) double cream
Crushed ice

Pour all the ingredients into a blender. Blend briefly at high speed until smooth. Start with a small amount of crushed ice and add more until you achieve the desired thickness. Pour into a glass of your choice and garnish with fresh raspberries.

Raspberries grow wild all over Northern Europe, but they are also cultivated commercially all year round. If you're looking for wild raspberries, try to find them where the landscape is a bit rocky and around forest clearings, which is where raspberry bushes thrive.

Strawberry Kiss

1 oz (30 ml) Amaretto
1 oz (30 ml) triple sec
3 strawberries
1 oz (30 ml) double cream
Crushed ice
Fresh strawberries for garnish

Pour all the ingredients into a blender. Blend briefly at high speed until smooth. Start with a small amount of crushed ice and add more until you achieve the desired thickness. Pour into a glass of your choice and garnish with fresh strawberries.

People who are allergic to red strawberries can eat a special sort of white strawberries that lack the red pigment.

Frozen Cappuccino

1 oz (30 ml) Baileys
½ oz (15 ml) Kahlúa
½ oz (15 ml) Frangelico
1 scoop vanilla ice-cream
Crushed ice

Pour all the ingredients into a blender. Blend briefly at high speed until smooth. Start with a small amount of crushed ice and add more until you achieve the desired thickness. Serve in a margarita glass. Dust a little cinnamon or cocoa powder on top.

Simply a dream when it's too hot for coffee...

Frozen Mango Sling

1 ½ oz (45 ml) Absolut Apeach
½ oz (15 ml) peach liqueur
½ oz (15 ml) lemon juice
½ oz (15 ml) simple syrup
1 diced mango
Crushed ice

Pour all the ingredients into a blender. Blend briefly at high speed until smooth. Start with a small amount of crushed ice and add more until you achieve the desired thickness. Serve in a highball glass and garnish with fresh mango.

Mango is the national fruit of India and Pakistan and is full of goodies including carotene and antioxidants, but it also contains urushiol, something it has in common Brazil nuts. Allergy sufferers should exercise some caution, at least when handling the peel.

Shots and Shooters

Shots are the shortest of all short drinks – they are downed in one swig. You barely have time to taste it, but it burns all the more on the way down! Shot drinking is extremely popular with some, but others see it as a waste of both money and fine spirits.

There is the classic image of downing shots, which is associated with old western movies, but shot drinking has been around for much longer – traces of ancient vessels used for imbibing shots have been found in China.

There are shots and there are shooters. A shot consists of a single type of liquor, whereas a shooter is a mini-cocktail in shot form, usually consisting of two or more spirits. These are often layered and can be tricky to get right, or at least that's what the bartender wants you to believe. This is how you conjure up a fancy layered drink that will earn you the epithet 'Wizard of Oz':

LAYERING
Start by pouring the first ingredient into a shot glass.

Pour the next ingredient slowly over the back of a spoon held close to the side of the glass. Repeat the procedure with the next liquid, and so on. The order is crucial, the heaviest liquid must go on the bottom or they will mix and the effect will be ruined.

A Manda Shot

1 oz (30 ml) Absolut Mandrin
Orange wedge
Grenadine, on a saucer
Caster sugar, on a saucer

Pour the vodka into a shot glass. Dip the orange wedge into the grenadine and then into the sugar. Let the orange wedge balance elegantly on top of the glass and serve. This should be drunk as a tequila shot – in one go followed by a bite into the orange.

This is the tutti-frutti version of a tequila shot – the more innocent sister of the tangy Lemon Drop Shot.

Bazooka

½ oz (15 ml) vodka
½ oz (15 ml) blue curaçao
½ oz (15 ml) milk
Cocoa powder for garnish

Pour the ingredients into a
shaker filled with ice. Shake
and strain into a shot glass.
Dust cocoa powder on top.

TIP! *For a more grown-up version:
replace the milk with Baileys. If you
want a green bazooka: replace the
vodka with banana liqueur. Both
versions are delicious as cocktails
too – simply double the amounts
and serve in a Martini glass.*

*A bazooka is a portable rocket launcher that was invented in the US during World War II. It was able to
stop tanks and penetrate bunker walls. A slightly violent way to get to a woman's heart in other words …*

Birdy Nam Nam

¼ oz (7 ml) vodka
¼ oz (7 ml) gin
¼ oz (7 ml) light rum
¼ oz (7 ml) Pisang Ambon

Pour the ingredients into a shaker filled with ice. Shake and strain into a shot glass.

TIP! *Pisang Ambon is delicious to drink on its own or drizzled over vanilla ice-cream.*

Pisang Ambon is an Indonesian liqueur with an exotic flavour. Its fruitiness includes clear hints of banana, which is perfect for when you start to long for turquoise water and swaying palm trees. Pisang is the Malay word for banana and Ambon is the Indonesian island where the banana plant was first discovered.

Adios Motherfucker

½ oz (15 ml) Kahlúa
½ oz (15 ml) tequila
Whole chilli pepper for
garnish

Layer each ingredient, in the
right order, in a shot glass.
Tricky? Read about layering
on page 160.

TIP! *Don't eat the garnish...*

*There are many different versions of Adios Motherfucker, some of which are long drinks with four or
five white spirits mixed with Sprite. These are better suited for a slow goodbye...*

B-52

⅓ oz (10 ml) Kahlúa
⅓ oz (10 ml) Baileys
⅓ oz (10 ml) Grand Marnier

Layered. Start by pouring the Kahlúa into a shot glass. Add the Baileys, carefully, over the back of a teaspoon to form a second layer on top of the Kahlúa. Proceed with the Grand Marnier. The order is crucial – the heaviest liquid goes on the bottom.

TIP! *Replace Grand Marnier with:*
1) *Vodka for a B-53*
2) *Amaretto for a B-54*
3) *Absinthe for a B-55*

The name of this shot is said to come from the first American bomber Boeing B-52 Stratofortress, which was used frequently during the Vietnam War. Set fire to your shot, and you have a 'crashing B-52' – quite a macabre image. Use a heatproof glass and replace the Grand Marnier with dark rum (60–80%). Flaming shots require a lot of precaution: be sure to have a wet towel or a bucket of water nearby.

Blow Job

⅓ oz (10 ml) Kahlúa
⅔ oz (20 ml) Baileys
Lightly whipped cream

Layered. Start by pouring the Kahlúa into a shot glass. Add the Baileys, carefully, over the back of a teaspoon to form a second layer on top of the Kahlúa. Proceed with the cream. The order is crucial; the heaviest liquid goes on the bottom.

TIP! *Reducing the amount of Baileys and replacing it with your favourite liqueur, for example banana liqueur, Cointreau or Amaretto is a tasty alternative.*

This is a playful party drink that should be drunk without using your hands: hold the glass with your mouth, tilt your head back and swallow. The cream will run down your chin!

Fast Bloody Mary

1 oz (30 ml) Absolut Pepper
1 tomato wedge
Salt on a saucer
Tiny celery stick for garnish

Pour the pepper vodka into a shot glass. Dip the tomato wedge in the salt. Balance the tomato wedge elegantly on top of the glass, next to the celery stick, and serve. This should be drunk as a tequila shot – first the vodka and then a bite into the tomato.

Could this be the world's fastest hangover cure?

Galliano Hot Shot

1 oz (30 ml) Galliano
1 oz (30 ml) coffee
Lightly whipped cream

Layered. Start by pouring the Galliano into a shot glass. Add the coffee, carefully, over the back of a teaspoon, to form a second layer on top of the Galliano. Proceed with the cream. The order is crucial – the heaviest liquid goes on the bottom.

This could be the world's smallest coffee drink. It was created by Swedish bartender Bo Bergström at a coffee drink contest in 1987. As a result of him choosing the (then) unknown liqueur Galliano in his new drink, the brand increased its sales by 750 per cent over the next six years.

Hot, Sweet & Spicy

1 oz (30 ml) Absolut Pepper
3 strawberries
4 basil leaves
Crushed ice

This is a frozen shot where the ingredients are mixed with crushed ice in an electric blender – a little at a time – until the desired thickness is achieved. Pour into a shot glass and garnish with chilli pepper.

TIP! *This shot is excellent as a cocktail too. Pour it into a Martini glass and take your time drinking it.*

Absolut Pepper was first introduced in 1986 as the perfect vodka for Bloody Maries. A new trend – flavoured vodka – was born there and then. Flavoured vodkas have inspired countless new cocktails and flavour sensations, even though puritanical vodka connoisseurs tend to consider them quite vulgar...

Lemon Drop Shot

1 oz (30 ml) vodka
1 oz (30 ml) lemon juice
Lemon wedge and caster
 sugar for garnish

Pour the vodka and lemon
juice into a shaker filled with
ice. Shake and strain into a
shot glass. Dip the lemon
wedge in sugar on both sides
and place it on top of the
glass. This should be drunk
as a tequila shot – in one go
followed by a bite into the
lemon.

A tangy sensation invented by the European president of the International Bartenders Association.
If you prefer sweeter stuff, try A Manda Shot instead.

Liquid Viagra

¾ oz (20 ml) Jägermeister
1 ½ oz (45 ml) Red Bull

Pour Jägermeister into a shot glass. Fill up with ice-cold Red Bull and shoot it down!

*Easy on the alcohol but loaded with energy
– suitable for a man with a plan...*

Paintball

½ oz (15 ml) crème de
  menthe, white or green
½ oz (15 ml) Baileys

Pour the crème de menthe
into a shot glass. Let the
Baileys form a layer on top by
pouring it carefully over the
back of a teaspoon.

Paintball is in fact one of the games which causes the least injuries.
Too much Paintball in liquid form, however, may result in quite a few injuries...

Screwdriver Shot

1 oz (30 ml) vodka
½ oz (15 ml) orange juice
Orange wedge

Pour the vodka, orange juice and ice into a mixing glass and use the smallest screwdriver in the world to stir. Strain into a shot glass and place an orange wedge on top. This should be drunk as a tequila shot – in one go followed by a bite into the orange.

A Screwdriver contains vodka and orange juice.
If you fancy more volume, try the elder Screwdriver brother.

Slippery Nipple

½ oz (15 ml) Sambuca
½ oz (15 ml) Baileys
1 drop grenadine

Start by pouring the Sambuca
into a shot glass. Add Baileys,
carefully, over the back of a
teaspoon, to form a second
layer on top of the Sambuca.
Grenadine goes in at the end.

TIP! *Dip a straw into a cup of
grenadine and seal the top of the
straw with your finger to trap a
drop of grenadine inside. Place the
straw on the bottom centre of the
shot glass and remove your finger
from the top of the straw to release
the grenadine.*

*A single drop has given its name to this shot, but what a drop indeed! Grenadine is a syrup, which is
often used to colour drinks, but also to add sweetness. It is so colourful and sweet that one drop will do.
On the other hand…all good things are — two?*

St. Patrick's Shooter

⅓ oz (10 ml) Grand Marnier
Rouge
⅓ oz (10 ml) green crème de
menthe
⅓ oz (10 ml) Baileys Mint
Chocolate

Start by carefully pouring
the Grand Marnier into a
shot glass. Add the crème
de menthe and allow it to
mix with the Grand Marnier.
Finally, add the Baileys carefully
over the back of a teaspoon
to form a second layer on
top. Tricky? Read more about
layering on page 160.

Every year on March 17, the Irish celebrate St. Patrick's Day by wearing something green.
Tradition allows you to pinch anyone not wearing green, so beware!

Tequila Slammer

1 oz (30 ml) tequila
1 oz (30 ml) Sprite

Pour both ingredients into a
shot glass. Cover the top of
the glass with your hand or
a tissue, lift it up and slam it
down on the counter. Drink it
in one go while it's still fizzy!

TIP! *A glass coaster on the bar
counter decreases the risk of your
shot glass shattering.*

*Use champagne instead of Sprite in your shot
and it becomes a Slammer Royale!*

Stars and Stripes

½ oz (15 ml) Grenadine
½ oz (15 ml) blue curaçao
Lightly whipped cream

Layered. Start by pouring the Grenadine into a shot glass. Add the blue curaçao, carefully, over the back of a teaspoon, to form a second layer on top of the Grenadine. Proceed with the cream. The order is crucial – the heaviest liquid goes on the bottom.

This little shot is named after the American flag on which the red and white stripes symbolise the original thirteen states. The flag originally included the flag of England in the top left corner. As of 1777, this field is filled with fifty stars instead – one for each state.

Long Drinks

'The secret to a long life is to stay busy, get plenty of exercise and don't drink too much. Then again, don't drink too little.'

Herman Smith-Johannsen

Long drinks are served in large glasses but still contain the same amount of alcohol as cocktails and short drinks: normally 1 or 2 oz. The difference is that the glass is filled up with something else, usually juice or a carbonated drink. In this way, the alcohol becomes more diluted, which is the whole idea behind the long drink – it should last long without being too intoxicating. It does not mean that you can make any short drink into a long drink simply by adding soda. The recipes are carefully composed to preserve each cocktail's unique character as either a short or a long drink. A Dry Martini mixed with lemonade would not exactly be 'licensed to kill'...

A long drink is a refreshing thirst quencher and the ultimate beach party drink on a hot summer day. It keeps cool better than a short drink since the glass is usually filled to the brim with ice cubes. This is not a way for the bartender to save on the mixer, it is to allow the ice cubes to keep each other cool. Two or three lonely ice cubes will melt quickly, thus diluting your long drink and making it watery.

Long drinks are made up of two parts. One part consists of the measured spirits, which are often shaken to mix the ingredients, and one part which is used to fill up the glass, which should be chilled. Carbonated drinks should never be shaken, unless you have a masochistic stroke and want to clean the whole kitchen afterwards.

In Finland, 'long drinks' are ready-mixed drinks sold in a can. These usually have quite a low alcohol content and taste nothing like the original mixed by a bartender.

Gin and Tonic, or GT, is probably the world's best-known long drink.

Absolut Amore

1 oz (30 ml) Absolut Citron
1 oz (30 ml) Bols Parfait Amour
¾ oz (20 ml) lemon juice
½ oz (15 ml) cranberry juice
Lemonade
Red berries for garnish

Pour the first four ingredients into a shaker filled with ice. Shake well and strain into an ice-filled highball glass. Fill up with lemonade and add some red berries.

Contains 'perfect love' in French. Just like real love, which means that it's sour and sweet at the same time due to the combination of vanilla-violet and citrus. Some people claim that if a couple drink Parfait Amour after a quarrel they will make up immediately.

Absolut Passion

1 oz (30 ml) Absolut Mandrin
1 oz (30 ml) Passoã
1 ½ oz (45 ml) lime juice
Lemonade
Lime wheel for garnish

Pour the first three
ingredients into an ice-filled
highball glass. Fill up with
lemonade and stir. Garnish
with a lime wheel.

*Absolut Vodka had its worldwide breakthrough in the 1980s, partly through the introduction of a
clear bottle inspired by old-fashioned medicine bottles, with the text printed directly on the glass. In
2008, the Swedish vodka brand was sold to French spirits giant Pernod Ricard, but the bottles are still
manufactured in Sweden.*

American Dream

1 oz (30 ml) bourbon
1 oz (30 ml) sour apple liqueur
Lemonade
Apple slice for garnish

Pour the first two ingredients into an ice-filled highball glass. Fill up with lemonade and stir. Garnish with an apple slice.

Of all American whiskeys, bourbon is the best known. The name 'bourbon' is derived from the county in Kentucky where it was first created. In order for a whiskey to be called bourbon, it must contain a minimum of 51% barley. Bourbon is always stored in brand new, charred oak casks, which by law can only be used once. Afterwards, they are often sold and shipped to Scotland where they are used for storing Scotch.

Absolut Raspberri

1 ½ oz (45 ml) Absolut
  Raspberri
½ oz (15 ml) raspberry liqueur
Lemonade
Fresh raspberries for garnish

Pour the first two ingredients
into an ice-filled highball
glass. Fill up with lemonade
and stir. Garnish with fresh
raspberries.

TIP! *Unless otherwise stated,
always use ice cubes rather than
crushed ice when preparing long
drinks. Make sure the glass is at
least half-filled with ice cubes. This
keeps the drink cold longer.*

*Raspberries are a health-boosting treat. They contain large amounts of an unusual type of antioxidants,
which are not found in any other fruit or vegetable in the world.*

Bahama Mama

1 ½ oz (45 ml) dark rum
½ oz (15 ml) banana liqueur
½ oz (15 ml) coconut syrup
1 oz (30 ml) pineapple juice
1 oz (30 ml) orange juice
3 dashes grenadine

Pour the ingredients into a shaker filled with ice. Shake well and strain into an ice-filled hurricane glass. Garnish with an exotic touch.

Like a trip to the Caribbean served in a glass. The colour of the rum differs depending on the age.
Dark rum is the oldest, but is seldom used in cocktails.

Black Cat

1 oz (30 ml) vodka
1 oz (30 ml) cherry brandy
Cranberry juice
Coca Cola

Pour the first two ingredients into a small ice-filled highball glass. Fill up with equal parts cranberry juice and coke. Stir.

TIP! *Is Cherry brandy tricky to come by? Use regular brandy and cherry syrup and you will end up with more or less the same result.*

Bad luck? Superstitious? This is a black cat that nobody would mind crossing their path. A perfect Halloween drink!

Blackberry Beast

1 ½ oz (45 ml) absinth
½ oz (15 ml) Crème de Mûre
1 oz (30 ml) cranberry juice
6 mint leaves
5 blackberries
2 tbsp blueberry puree
1 tsp demerara sugar
Champagne

Muddle the blackberries, mint leaves and sugar in a shaker. Fill up with a scoop of crushed ice and add absinth, Crème de Mûre, puree and cranberry juice. Shake well. Strain into a highball glass and fill up with more crushed ice. Top with champagne and stir gently. Garnish with mixed berries.

Judging by the long list of ingredients, this mixture may appear slightly mad. And what about the absinth? Doesn't it drive you insane? No, research shows that the old recipe only contained harmless amounts of the toxic substance, which suggests that the monstrous effects were due to nothing but sheer drunkenness. This cocktail is indeed a bit of a beast, but definitely worth the trouble!

Bloody Devil

2 oz (60 ml) pepper vodka
5 oz (150 ml) tomato juice
2 dashes Tabasco
1 dash Worcestershire sauce
½ oz (15 ml) lemon juice
¼ tsp celery salt
Grated horseradish
Black pepper
Fresh chilli for garnish

Pour the first six ingredients into a shaker filled with ice. Shake well and strain into an ice-filled highball glass. Top with grated horseradish and black pepper. Garnish with a whole chilli pepper.

The Worcestershire sauce was originally developed in India in 1837 by Colonel Marcus Sandy.
It contains vinegar, molasses, tamarind, garlic, oriental spices and anchovies.

Bloody Mary

2 oz (60 ml) vodka
1 dash Worcestershire sauce
¼ tsp salt
¼ tsp pepper
½ oz (15 ml) lemon juice
2 dashes Tabasco
Tomato juice
Celery stick for garnish

Pour the first six ingredients into an ice-filled highball glass. Fill up with tomato juice and stir. Garnish with a celery stick.

Best known as the world's number one hangover cure – perhaps due to its saltiness. Many believe that this cocktail was named after Mary I, the bloodthirsty queen of England who was known for her many executions. A more likely story involves Pete Petiot, bartender at Harry's New York Bar in Paris and a Mary Pickford fan. Mary Pickford was a silent movie star known as 'the whole world's little sweetheart'. 'Bloody' would then refer to the drink's colour.

Blue Hawaiian

1 oz (30 ml) light rum
½ oz (15 ml) blue curaçao
½ oz (15 ml) Malibu
3 oz (100 ml) pineapple juice

Pour all the ingredients into a shaker filled with ice. Shake well and strain into an ice-filled highball glass.

TIP! *As this cocktail is related to Piña Colada, it can also be made with coconut milk instead of Malibu and blended in the same way as for the other members of the Piña family.*

Blue Hawaii is a 1961 film starring Elvis Presley. 'Can't Help Falling in Love' from the soundtrack was awarded the 1990 ASCAP Award for most performed song.

Cherry Julep

1 ½ oz (45 ml) gin
½ oz (15 ml) cherry brandy
½ oz (15 ml) lemon juice
Soda water
Maraschino cherries for garnish

Pour the first three ingredients into an ice-filled highball glass. Fill up with soda water and stir. Garnish with a maraschino cherry.

This popular American version of a Julep has few similarities with its 'mother', Mint Julep.
Julab is a 'soothing drink' in Arabic. It's a perfect description of both variations!

Casino

1 ½ oz (45 ml) gin
½ oz (15 ml) white maraschino
  liqueur
2 dashes Angostura Orange
  Bitter
½ oz (15 ml) lemon juice
Soda water

Pour the first four ingredients
into an ice-filled highball glass.
Fill up with soda water and
stir. Garnish with a party-like
touch.

TIP! *There are many different
versions of the Casino cocktail,
including this long drink. Skip the
soda if you prefer a shorter trip to
the casino.*

*Angostura Bitter is made according to a secret recipe concocted by the descendants of a German
doctor, Johann Siegert. During a trip to Venezuela in 1824, Mr. Siegert mixed the fever medicine meant
for the native Americans with spirit...*

Chill Out

1 oz (30 ml) light rum
1 oz (30 ml) Cointreau
Bitter lemon
Fresh chilli and lime for garnish

Pour the rum and liqueur into an ice-filled highball glass. Fill up with bitter lemon and stir. Cut chilli and lime into small pieces and drop them into the glass as garnish.

This cocktail was awarded first prize at the Havana Club Grand Prix, an international cocktail contest, in the year 2000. The bitterness of the bitter lemon mixer comes from the quinine, which was often used to combat malaria until the 1940s when new medicines were invented. It is still used in some medical emergencies. Quinine is extracted from the bark of the Cinchona tree.

Gin and Tonic

2 oz (60 ml) gin
Tonic water

Pour the gin into an ice-filled
highball glass. Fill up with
tonic water and stir. Garnish
with lemon or a lime wheel.

TIP! *For a sweeter Gin and Tonic,
use grape tonic instead.*

This is classic, if there ever was one, and many people's first contact with a real long drink.

Chartreuse and Tonic

2 oz (60 ml) Chartreuse
Tonic water
Fresh herbs for garnish

Pour the Chartreuse into an ice-filled highball glass. Fill up with tonic water and stir. Garnish with one of the 130 herbs that are part of the Chartreuse liqueur, which means that you have to convince the monks in Grenoble to reveal their secret 400-year-old recipe. Good luck!

A refreshing, green summer drink made with secret herbs.
According to rumour, one of them is angelica.

Cinnamon Liz

1 ½ oz (45 ml) vodka
½ oz Licor 43
Cinnamon
Apple juice

Dust an empty highball glass with cinnamon. Add ice cubes and pour in the liqueur and vodka. Fill up with apple juice and stir gently. Garnish with apple slices and serve with a straw.

Cinnamon is called cannella in Italian, which means 'small pipe'. It is made from the bark of a certain tree that grows in Sri Lanka and was well-known by the Egyptians as early as 1500 BC.

Cucumber Delight

1 ½ oz (45 ml) pear vodka
½ oz (15 ml) elderflower
 liqueur
1 oz (30 ml) freshly squeezed
 cucumber juice
½ oz (15 ml) lemon juice
1 tsp sugar
Splash of soda

Pour the first five ingredients
into a shaker filled with ice.
Shake well and strain into a
highball glass filled with ice
cubes. Top with soda and stir.

TIP! *Add a dash of green curaçao
for a deeper shade of green.*

*The cucumber is actually a fruit from India. It contains as much as 90% water, and its mild taste has
led many to believe that it lacks nutrients, which is somewhat unfair. It is relatively rich in vitamin C; one
serving contains 10% of your recommended daily intake.*

Collins

2 oz (60 ml) base spirit of
  choice
1 oz (30 ml) lemon juice
½ oz (15 ml) simple syrup
Soda water
Lemon for garnish

Pour the first three
ingredients into an ice-filled
highball glass. Fill up with soda
and stir. Garnish with lemon.

TIP! *Base spirits generally
include vodka, gin, rum, tequila,
whisky and brandy. Which is your
favourite Collins brother? We like
Tom, because we have a thing for
celebrities...*

*The only thing that separates a Collins from a Fizz is the amount of soda water. Sour is their cousin,
which is served without soda. In all other respects they are alike and share the same basic formula:
base spirit + sweet + sour. Meet the Collins brothers: The sweet Tom Collins made with (Old Tom) gin
is the most famous; John Collins, made with genever or London Dry Gin (a fickle fellow), appeared in a
recipe book as early as in 1892; Jack Collins is made with Scotch; Pierre Collins with brandy...*

Blackberry Collins

2 oz (60 ml) blackberry vodka
1 oz (30 ml) lemon juice
½ oz (15 ml) simple syrup
Soda water

Pour the first three ingredients into an ice-filled highball glass. Fill up with soda and stir.

TIP! *Do you know the Collins, Fizz and Sour families? Fizz is essentially a Collins, but with less soda. If you want no soda at all, make yourself a sour instead, the tangiest of the three cousins...*

Collins continued... Pedro Collins is made with rum, Mike Collins with Irish whiskey, Colonel Collins with bourbon, Captain Collins with Canadian whisky, Joe Collins with vodka, Jack Collins with applejack and Pepito Collins with tequila. Phew, spending time with all of them at once may prove fatal. A fruity Joe Collins, like above, is perhaps a bit unusual. Serve it in a Collins glass if you have one!

Cranberry Collins

2 oz (60 ml) cranberry vodka
1 oz (30 ml) lemon juice
½ oz (15 ml) simple syrup
Soda water
Fresh cranberries for garnish

Pour the first three
ingredients into an ice-filled
highball glass. Fill up with
soda and stir. Garnish with
cranberries.

TIP! *Achieve a nice colour effect by
adding a few dashes of grenadine
after stirring.*

*The name cranberry derives from 'craneberry'. This was the original name given by early European
settlers in North America who thought that the flower, stem, calyx and petals of the cranberry bush
reminded them of the neck, head and bill of a crane.*

Raspberry Collins

1 ½ oz (45 ml) gin
½ oz raspberry liqueur
1 oz (30 ml) lemon juice
½ oz (15 ml) simple syrup
Soda water
Fresh raspberries for garnish

Pour the first four ingredients
into an ice-filled highball glass.
Fill up with soda and stir.
Garnish with raspberries.

TIP! *Make a simpler version
without the liqueur and raspberries
by adding raspberry cordial and
double the amount of lemon juice
– it's a tasty alternative.*

*According to some sources, gin was invented by a Dutch pharmacist as early as in the 16th century.
The Dutch used to drink their 'genever' on the battlefield in order to relieve pain the fear of dying. It
made them feel invincible. The British admired their courage and began importing genever for the same
purpose. They later began producing their own version – gin!*

Cucumber GT

2 oz (60 ml) gin
½ oz (15 ml) lime juice
Cucumber sticks
Tonic water

Pour the gin and lime juice
into a highball glass. Add the
cucumber sticks and fill up
with tonic.

TIP! *Feel free to eat the garnish
afterwards.*

*In March 1998, the British tabloid The Sun reported that, according to new EU rules, 'Cucumbers have
to be straight and must not arch more than 10 mm for every 10 mm of their length so people can tell
how many are in a box'. This was later revealed as a misunderstanding.*

Enok

1 oz (30 ml) light rum
½ oz (15 ml) raspberry liqueur
½ oz (15 ml) Cointreau
½ oz (15 ml) lime juice
Tonic water

Pour the first four ingredients into a shaker filled with ice. Shake well and strain into a highball glass filled with ice cubes. Fill up with tonic and stir. Garnish with red berries and lime.

In the Caribbean in the 17th century, someone discovered that sugar cane juice can be used for making spirits. This new spirit was called the 'kill devil' or 'rumbaillon'. The latter explains the drink's modern-day name, rum.

Fidel Castro

2 oz (60 ml) dark rum
3 lime wedges
Ginger ale
Diced apple

Squeeze the lime into an
ice-filled highball glass and
add the wedges as decoration.
Add the diced apple and rum.
Fill up with ginger ale.

*Fidel Castro, who seized power in Cuba after the 1959 revolution and remained president until 2008,
had this cocktail created in his honour. Perhaps he did not even knot it contains an American soft drink!*

Cuba Libre

2 oz (60 ml) light rum
2 lime wedges
Coca Cola

Pour rum into an ice-filled highball glass. Squeeze the juice out of the lime wedges and add the wedges as decoration. Fill up with coke and stir.

This 'drink of liberty' was created when the U.S. fought against the Spaniards in Cuba to free the country from Spanish colonial rule. A thirsty American captain is said to have walked into a Cuban bar in 1893 and asked the bartender to mix the Coca Cola he had brought with him with rum. Soon, all the homesick American soldiers at the surrounding tables started to ask for the same. They all raised their glasses and exclaimed: 'To a free Cuba!'

Fizz Lemon

2 oz (60 ml) base spirit of
  choice
1 oz (30 ml) lemon juice
½ oz (15 ml) simple syrup
Splash of soda

Pour all the ingredients
except the soda into a shaker
filled with ice. Shake well
and strain into an ice-filled
highball glass. Top with soda.
Garnish with a lemon wedge
and serve with a straw.

*The Collins, Fizz and Sour families are all made using the same basic recipe. A Fizz is in fact a Collins
with a little less soda. If you prefer your Collins without soda altogether, make yourself a Sour, the
tangiest of the three cousins. The base spirits used are the most common cocktail-making spirits usually
vodka, gin, rum, tequila, whisky or brandy.*

Fizz Pomegranate

2 oz (60 ml) pomegranate
  vodka
1 oz (30 ml) lemon juice
½ oz (15 ml) simple syrup
Splash of soda

Pour all the ingredients
except the soda into a shaker
filled with ice. Shake well
and strain into an ice-filled
highball glass. Top with soda.
Serve with a straw.

*Fizz Lemon is the 'patriarch' of the Fizz family. Another option is to make
yourself a Silver Fizz by adding whipped egg white to the basic recipe.
To make a Golden Fizz, replace the egg white with egg yolk...*

Fizz Orange

1 ½ oz (45 ml) tequila
½ oz (15 ml) Cointreau
½ oz (15 ml) lemon juice
½ oz (15 ml) simple syrup
Splash of soda

Pour all the ingredients
except the soda into a shaker
filled with ice. Shake well
and strain into an ice-filled
highball glass. Top with soda.
Garnish with a wedge of
blood orange and serve with
a straw.

*A Fizz is often served in a smaller glass than the traditional highball since it does not contain as much
soda as drinks from the Collins family. In other respects, Fizz and Collins are the same drink: a base
spirit combined with lemon and simple syrup and filled up with soda. Feel free to add liqueurs and
experiment, as we have done here.*

Fizz Green

1 ½ oz (45 ml) vodka
½ oz (15 ml) white Crème de Menthe
½ oz (15 ml) lemon juice
½ oz (15 ml) simple syrup
Splash of soda

Pour all the ingredients except the soda into a shaker filled with ice. Shake well and strain into an ice-filled highball glass. Top with soda. Serve with a straw.

Peppermint belongs to the mint family. The leaves are pressed to extract mint oil, which mainly consists of menthol. The English love spearmint, or green mint. It is used in sweets and to make the mint sauce that goes with roast lamb.

Wasp's Nest

1 ½ oz (45 ml) vodka
½ oz (15 ml) banana liqueur
Ginger ale

Pour the ingredients into
an ice-filled highball glass.
Fill up with ginger ale and
stir. Garnish with a twist of
orange or lemon peel.

This is a banana-flavoured, sweet and yellow creation with a sting!

Grenade

2 oz (60 ml) pomegranate
  vodka
½ oz (15 ml) lime juice
Lemonade
Pomegranate seeds for garnish

Pour the ingredients into an
ice-filled highball glass. Fill
up with lemonade and stir.
Garnish with pomegranate
seeds.

*Are you finding it tricky to get the tasty pomegranate seeds out? Try rolling the pomegranate against a
flat surface to loosen the seeds. Split it in half. Hold one half upside down and beat it with the back of
a wooden spoon – and voilà – the seeds come falling out.*

Grand Passion

1 oz (30 ml) watermelon liqueur
1 oz (30 ml) Passoã
1 oz (30 ml) water melon syrup
½ passion fruit
2 lime wedges
1 watermelon wedge
Sprite

Muddle the passion fruit,
watermelon and lime wedges
in a shaker. Fill up with crushed
ice and add the liqueurs and
syrup. Shake well and strain
into a hurricane glass. Fill up
with more crushed ice and top
with Sprite.

The passion fruit belongs to the passion flower family, a very large genus of more than 500 species. A few of the family members are a bit shady – some are said to contain hallucinogens. However, if this drink should cause you to hallucinate, it probably has more to do with the alcohol than with the fruit...

Green Envy

2 oz (60 ml) lemon vodka
2 dashes green curaçao
Sprite
Lime for garnish

Pour the vodka and liqueur into an ice-filled highball glass. Fill up with Sprite and stir. Garnish with lime slices.

Curaçao is a very popular liqueur that is also used for making Crêpes Suzette.

Love in an Elevator

1 oz (30 ml) gin
1 oz (30 ml) green curaçao
Ginger ale

Pour the gin and liqueur into an ice-filled highball glass. Fill up with ginger ale and stir.

The reason for the name of this drink is obscure. Some say it has to do with the fact that it was originally garnished with raisins that would bob up and down in the glass like elevators. Today, it is rarely served with raisins, which have been replaced by a maraschino cherry or a slice of lemon.

Havana Hot Nights

1 ½ oz (45 ml) Havana Club
  Añejo 7 Años
½ oz (15 ml) pear brandy
2 dashes Galliano
Ginger ale
Mint leaves for garnish

Pour the rum and pear brandy into an ice-filled highball glass together with some mint leaves. Fill up with ginger ale and top with Galliano.

Havana Club 7 Años is sometimes called 'the pride of Cuba'.
Here you find it in the pleasant company of pear, aniseed, ginger and mint.

Horse's Neck

2 oz (60 ml) brandy
Ginger ale
2 dashes Angostura Bitter
Lemon for garnish

Pour the brandy into an ice-filled highball glass. Fill up with ginger ale and stir. Finish off by adding a few dashes of Angostura if desired.

Garnish: Use a channel knife or a potato peeler to create a long spiral of lemon peel and drape it in the glass to resemble a curved horse's neck.

TIP! *Replace the brandy with bourbon to create a Stiff Horse's Neck, also known as an American Horse's Neck. Or use Scotch for a Scotch Horse's Neck.*

The elegantly coiled lemon peel in this cocktail is meant to remind us of the beautiful arched neck of a horse. In the late 1800s, Horse's Neck was a non-alcoholic drink. When alcohol was added to the recipe around 1910 – bourbon originally– it was renamed Horse's Neck with a Kick. Over the years, the alcohol-free version fell into oblivion, and the non-alcoholic variant lost half its name – but the contents still give you a kick!

Indo

1 oz (30 ml) Bacardi Lemon
1 oz (30 ml) Sourz Peach
Lemonade

Pour the rum and liqueur into an ice-filled highball glass. Fill up with lemonade and stir. Garnish with a lemon wheel.

Rum is usually made with molasses. , a thick, syrupy by-product of the processing of sugar cane into sugar. It consists of about 50% sugar and has a dark brown colour. It contains minerals and beneficial micronutrients. Along with dried carrots and bran, it is also a delicious snack for horses. Molasses before they have been distilled that is — not rum!

Alaska Iced Tea

½ oz (15 ml) vodka
½ oz (15 ml) gin
½ oz (15 ml) light rum
½ oz (15 ml) Cointreau
½ oz (15 ml) blue curaçao
Lemonade

Pour all the ingredients into
an ice-filled highball glass. Fill
up with lemonade and stir.

*Gin, rum or vodka? Why not try all of them at once? Typically, a long drink contains no more than one
of the base spirits above. The Long Island family, however, usually break this pattern, making it the
perfect drink for the indecisive. Here is an unusually successful and stylish blue combination where the
different spirits balance each other perfectly. See also the original – Long Island Iced Tea.*

Bangkok Iced Tea

½ oz (15 ml) vodka
½ oz (15 ml) gin
½ oz (15 ml) light rum
½ oz (15 ml) red vermouth
½ oz (15 ml) lime juice
Ginger ale
Red chilli pepper and coriander
   for garnish

Pour all the ingredients into
an ice-filled highball glass or
a large wine glass. Fill up with
ginger ale and stir. Garnish
with chilli and coriander.

In Bangkok, a highly-alcoholic Iced Tea is not good enough.
It has to be spicy too!

Beverly Hills Iced Tea

½ oz (15 ml) vodka
½ oz (15 ml) gin
½ oz (15 ml) light rum
½ oz (15 ml) tequila
½ oz (15 ml) lemon juice
Sparkling wine
2 dashes of triple sec

Pour all the ingredients
except the triple sec and
sparkling wine into an ice-
filled highball glass. Fill up with
sparkling wine and stir. Top
with triple sec and garnish
with something party-like.

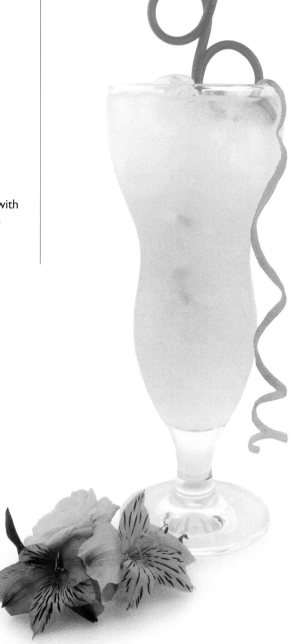

*This elegant version of the classic Long Island Iced Tea suitably contains champagne instead of coca
cola. You immediately feel the urge to put on high heels and a matching hat...*

Irish Iced Tea

2 oz (60 ml) Irish whiskey
½ oz (15 ml) lime juice
Peach iced tea

Pour the whiskey and lime juice into an ice-filled tumbler. Fill up with iced tea and stir.

An Iced Tea that in fact contains iced tea is unusual. Then again, this isn't a proper Iced Tea, as it only contains one type of spirit. It's delicious all the same!

Italian Iced Tea

2 oz (60 ml) Martini Rosso
½ oz (15 ml) orange juice
½ oz (15 ml) lemon juice
½ oz (15 ml) lime juice
Ginger ale
Orange peel for garnish

Pour the first four ingredients
into an ice-filled highball glass
and stir. Fill up with ginger ale.
Garnish with orange peel.

*This is an Iced Tea with a more moderate alcohol content, which can also be made in a pitcher and
served to thirsty guests on a lovely summer evening. Simply mix 8 oz (250 ml) of Martini Rosso with
16 oz (500 ml) of ginger ale and 4 oz (120 ml) of each of the fruit juices. Add pieces of fruit.*

Long Beach Iced Tea

½ oz (15 ml) vodka
½ oz (15 ml) gin
½ oz (15 ml) light rum
½ oz (15 ml) tequila
½ oz (15 ml) lemon juice
Cranberry juice
⅓ oz (10 ml) Cointreau

Pour all the ingredients except the Cointreau into an ice-filled highball glass. Fill up with cranberry juice and stir. Top with Cointreau.

Cranberry juice is a popular drinks mixer found in each and every cocktail nowadays, which calls for its very own Iced Tea.

Long Island Iced Tea

½ oz (15 ml) vodka
½ oz (15 ml) gin
½ oz (15 ml) light rum
½ oz (15 ml) tequila
½ oz (15 ml) lemon juice
½ oz (15 ml) Cointreau
Coca Cola

Pour all the ingredients
except the Coca Cola into
an ice-filled highball glass. Fill
up with Coca Cola and stir.
Garnish with lemon.

This is not as innocent as it sounds. An unusually strong long drink usually contains four or more different clear spirits. This is the creation of bartender Robert C 'Rosebud' Butt, who first mixed this beast of a drink in the late 1970s and named it after its place of origin, the Oak Beach Inn at Hampton Bays, Long Island. He added 'iced tea' as this was what the result reminded him of. Over the years, the Iced Tea family has grown to include many different variants of the old classic.

1 oz (30 ml) vanilla vodka
1 oz (30 ml) sour apple liqueur
½ oz (15 ml) lime juice
Lemonade

Pour all the ingredients except the lemonade into a shaker filled with ice. Shake well and strain into an ice-filled highball glass. Fill up with lemonade and stir.

Vanilla is delicious, but the spice's breakthrough in Europe had other causes. It was believed to improve male potency. This led to a major breakthrough of vanilla in Europe in the 18th century. Some men went so far as to stuff their pipes with tobacco mixed with vanilla seeds...

Lennart

2 oz (60 ml) pear brandy
1 oz (30 ml) lime or lemon
  juice
Sprite

Pour the brandy and citrus
juice into an ice-filled highball
glass. Fill up with Sprite and
stir. Garnish with lemon.

*Lennart and Ragnar are two Swedish long drink cousins that have entered the international cocktail
scene in recent years. The family has a few more cousins: Nisse, who prefers Absolut Mandrin, and
Pekka, who likes Finlandia Cranberry. In all other respects, the drinks are alike.*

Ragnar

2 oz (60 ml) Absolut Kurant
1 oz (30 ml) lime juice
Lemonade

Pour the vodka and lime juice into an ice-filled highball glass. Fill up with lemonade and stir. Garnish with lime.

TIP! *To make a Ragnhild, use half the amount of Absolut Kurant and 1 oz of raspberry rum instead.*

Ragnar has quite a few male relatives.
Read about them under Lennart!

Lynchburg Lemonade

1 oz (30 ml) Jack Daniel's
1 oz (30 ml) triple sec
1 oz (30 ml) lemon juice
Lemonade

Pour the first three ingredients into an ice-filled highball glass. Fill up with lemonade and stir. Garnish with lime.

Lynchburg Lemonade is a highly popular long drink created by Jack Daniel's. The distillery is located in the city of Lynchburg, Tennessee – hence the name.

Mango Lemonade

1 ½ oz (45 ml) spicy dark rum
½ oz (15 ml) Malibu Mango
1 oz (30 ml) lemon juice
½ oz (15 ml) simple syrup
3 oz (90 ml) mango juice
1 physalis

Pour all the liquid ingredients into an ice-filled highball glass and stir. Garnish with the physalis.

Not only does mango play a leading role in chutney; it has become a trendy ingredient in juices and other beverages too, almost surpassing peaches in popularity.

Madras

2 oz (60 ml) vodka
2 oz (60 ml) orange juice
2 oz (60 ml) cranberry juice

Pour all ingredients into a shaker filled with ice. Shake well and strain into an ice-filled highball glass.

This refreshing, highly popular highball drink was named after an old colonial town in India, which is today better known as Chennai.

Caribbean Madras

2 oz (60 ml) dark rum
2 oz (60 ml) orange juice
2 oz (60 ml) cranberry juice

Pour all the ingredients into a shaker filled with ice. Shake well and strain into an ice-filled highball glass.

Somebody has spilt a splash of rum in the
Indian Madras to create a Caribbean Madras.

Mandarin Delight

1 ½ oz (45 ml) Absolut Mandrin
½ oz (15 ml) Cointreau
½ oz (15 ml) lime juice
Tonic water

Pour the first three
ingredients into a shaker filled
with ice. Shake well and strain
into an ice-filled highball glass.
Fill up with tonic and stir.

Tonic water contains quinine, which was once used to treat malaria.
Another cool side-effect is that becomes fluorescent in UV-light.

Mai Tai

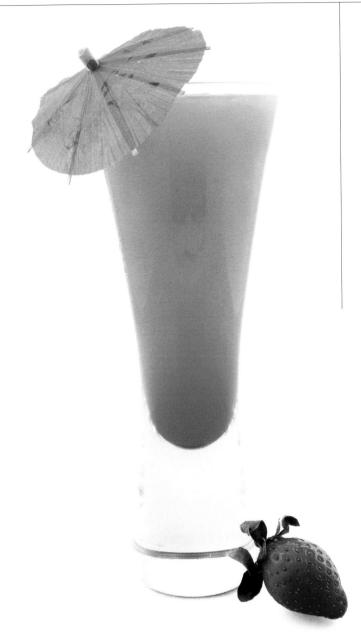

½ oz (15 ml) dark rum
½ oz (15 ml) light rum
½ oz (15 ml) Cointreau
½ oz (15 ml) amaretto
½ oz (15 ml) lime juice
2 oz (60 ml) orange juice
2 oz (60 ml) pineapple juice
2 dashes grenadine

Pour all the ingredients except the grenadine into a shaker filled with ice. Shake well and strain into an ice-filled highball glass. Add the grenadine and garnish with a parasol to protect the drink from the tropical sun...

Victor 'Trader Vic' Bergeron was experimenting with a new drink at his bar in Oakland, California. He used his friends Ham and Carrie Guild from Tahiti as advisers. Suddenly Carrie exclaimed: 'Mai tai, roe ae!' – 'The best! Divine!' in Tahitian. The year was 1944, 'Trader Vic' became famous, and today the whole world can gratefully enjoy 'the best' cocktail.

Mojito

2 oz (60 ml) light rum
½ lime
½ oz (15 ml) simple syrup
6 mint leaves
Soda water

Muddle the lime, mint leaves
and syrup gently in a highball
glass. Fill up with crushed ice,
add rum and stir. Fill up with
soda. Serve with a straw and
garnish with a sprig of mint.

*Mintha was a beautiful nymph in Greek mythology who fell in love with Hades, the god of death.
As the love was reciprocated, Hades' wife Persephone became furious and stamped the poor
nymph to death transforming her into dust. Hades caused the mint plant to grow forth from
the dust. It had the same intense impact on the world as the poor girl once had.
We now continue to smash and beat the life out of her...*

Apple Mojito

2 oz (60 ml) Bacardi Apple
1 oz (30 ml) lime cordial
½ lime
½ oz (15 ml) simple syrup
6 mint leaves
Soda water
Diced apple for garnish

Muddle the lime, mint leaves and syrup gently in a highball glass. Fill up with crushed ice, add rum and stir. Fill up with soda and add diced apple. Serve with a straw.

Ever since the Mojito recipe was invented in Cuba nearly 100 years ago, a series of variations have seen the light of day. Whatever the variant, true Mojito puritans detest crushed ice and do not want it anywhere near their Mojitos.

Orange Mojito

1 oz (30 ml) light rum
½ oz (15 ml) Absolut Mandrin
½ oz (15 ml) Mandarine
  Napoléon
½ lime
2 orange wedges
½ oz (15 ml) simple syrup
6 mint leaves
Soda water

Muddle the lime, orange, mint leaves and syrup gently in a highball glass. Fill up with crushed ice, add rum, vodka and liqueur and stir. Fill up with soda and serve with a straw.

TIP! *Instead of using plain light rum, try Bacardi for a more intense citrus flavour.*

The Cuban long drink Mojito is said to be the world's oldest cocktail. Its predecessor, El Draque, which dates back to the 16th century, contained tafia (a predecessor to rum), mint leaves, lime and sugar – more or less like our modern-day Mojito. There are countless variations of the Mojito, this one offers fresh citrus notes and a touch of vodka.

Pomegranate Mojito

2 oz (60 ml) light rum
1 oz (30 ml) pomegranate juice
½ lime
2 chunks pomegranate
½ oz (15 ml) simple syrup
6 mint leaves
Soda water

Muddle the pomegranate, lime, mint leaves and syrup gently in a highball glass. Fill up with crushed ice, add rum and juice and stir. Fill up with soda and serve with a straw.

The delicious, red juice is extracted from the pulp of the pomegranate. It is used for making the highly popular cocktail ingredient grenadine.

Thai Mojito

2 oz (60 ml) Havana Club
  Añejo Reserva
½ lime
1 tsp demerara sugar
½ oz (15 ml) ginger juice
6 coriander leaves
1 chilli for garnish

Muddle the lime, coriander, sugar and half of the chilli in a tumbler. Fill up the glass with crushed ice, add rum and stir. Serve with a straw and garnish with chilli and coriander leaves.

Fresh grated ginger is used in much the same way as dried ginger, but it is juicier and crisper. Ginger was first brought to Northern Europe by the Romans, and it was one of the most popular spices of the Middle Ages.

Joe Loudmouth

2 oz (60 ml) tequila
2 orange wedges
3 lime wedges
4–6 mint leaves
½ oz (15 ml) simple syrup
Soda water

Muddle the orange, lime, mint leaves and syrup gently in a highball glass. Fill up with crushed ice, add tequila and stir. Fill up with soda and serve with a straw.

This is very close to a Margarita, except for the refreshing mint leaves.
According to rumour, it was named after an unusually loud bartender.

Moulin Rouge

1 oz (30 ml) honey vodka
½ oz (15 ml) Crème de Mûre
½ oz (15 ml) macadamia nut
 liqueur
10 raspberries, a few for garnish
1 lemon wedge
Lemonade (optional)

Muddle the raspberries and
lemon in a shaker. Add vodka
and liqueurs. Shake well
and strain into an ice-filled
highball glass. Add a splash of
lemonade if desired and some
raspberries for garnish.

TIP! *There are several variants
of the Moulin Rouge cocktail. The
following recipe contains ingredients
that may be easier to come by:
1 oz Pernod Absinthe, cranberry
juice, mint leaves. (Absinthe has an
alcohol content of 68 per cent, so
1 oz is enough.)*

*The famous Paris cabaret Moulin Rouge was most famous for its cancan dancers. The tragic musical
with the same name – a love story between the beautiful but critically ill dancer and courtesan Satine
(Nicole Kidman) and a young poet, Christian (Ewan McGregor) – was released in 2001 and is set in
Paris in the early 20th century. The film gave rise to a new fashion trend with corsets and lace that has
still not worn off.*

Moscow Mule

2 oz (60 ml) vodka
2–3 limes
Ginger beer or ginger ale

Muddle the lime gently in a highball glass. Fill up with ice cubes and add the vodka. Fill up with ice-cold ginger beer.

In 1941, Jack Morgan, owner of The Cock 'n' Bull saloon in Los Angeles, found himself with too much ginger beer in stock. Smirnoff business man John Martin wanted to get rid of their copper mugs with mule motifs. The solution to the problem was Moscow Mule. The name refers to the Russian origins of vodka and the mule-like kick you get from ginger beer.

Green Man

1 oz (60 ml) vodka
1 oz (60 ml) melon liqueur
Sprite

Pour the vodka and liqueur into an ice-filled highball glass and stir. Fill up with Sprite and serve with a straw.

TIP! *For a more ice-cream-like feeling, use crushed ice instead of ice cubes, or use milk instead of Sprite.*

The Green Man is a refreshing summer treat with a childlike flavour combination

Pink Summer

2 oz (60 ml) gin
½ oz (15 ml) lime juice
Schweppes Russchian

Fill a highball glass with ice
cubes and the lime juice.
Add the gin and fill up with
Schweppes Russchian. Garnish
with lime.

Schweppes has been a well-known beverage brand since 1783
and is said to have invented the soft drink.

Ruby Red

1 ½ oz (45 ml) vodka
½ oz (15 ml) Campari
Grapefruit juice

Pour the vodka and Campari
into an ice-filled highball glass.
Fill up with grapefruit juice
and stir.

*This is one of the drinks that became popular through the Sex and the City television sitcom (the girls
simply couldn't drink Cosmopolitan in every episode). Ruby Red is made with blood grapefruit, but
ordinary yellow grapefruit juice is an excellent substitute.*

Passion

1 ½ oz (45 ml) vodka
½ oz (15 ml) Passoã
2 oz (60 ml) passion fruit juice
½ passion fruit
Sprite

Muddle the passion fruit in a
shaker. Fill up with ice-cubes,
add the rest of the ingredients
except the Sprite and shake
well. Strain into a highball
glass, add crushed ice and fill
up with Sprite.

*This popular fruit is known by many names: Granadilla (South America and South Africa),
Pasiflora (Israel), Parchita (Venezuela), Maracujá (Brazil, Ecuador, Peru, Paraguay)
and Lilikoi (Hawaii), to mention a few.*

Salty Dog

2 oz (60 ml) vodka
Grapefruit juice
Salt rim and grapefruit wedge
  for garnish

Pour the vodka into an ice-
filled highball glass. Fill up
with grapefruit juice and stir.
Garnish with salt on the rim
and a grapefruit wedge.

Salt rim: Pour some salt
onto a saucer. Moisten
the rim of the glass with a
grapefruit wedge and dip the
upturned glass into the salt.

TIP! *Hold the glass upside-down
while moistening it to avoid the juice
running down the glass.*

*Grapefruits do not grow wild. The fruit was discovered at some point during
the 18th century in a West Indian citrus plantation. Thank heavens for that!*

San Francisco

1 ½ oz (45 ml) vodka
½ oz (15 ml) banana liqueur
½ oz (15 ml) grenadine
Orange juice

Pour the vodka and liqueur
into a shaker filled with ice.
Shake well and strain into an
ice-filled highball glass. Fill up
with orange juice and top
with grenadine. Garnish with
an orange slice.

TIP! *Why not add some apricot
liqueur too for a change?*

This is an old, popular classic based on orange juice.

Sangria

Serves 10–15

2 bottles sweet Spanish red wine
4 oz (120 ml) Cointreau
3 oz (90 ml) brandy
3 oz (90 ml) orange juice
2 oz (60 ml) lemon juice
2 oz (60 ml) lime juice
8 oz (240 ml) simple syrup
Orange slices
Lemon slices
Lime slices
Grapes

Pour all the liquid ingredients into a large bowl (or two pitchers) and give everything a good stir. Add a pint of ice cubes and the fruit.

TIP! *Sangria is a type of Spanish punch to which all sorts of fruits and berries can be added. Try replacing the oranges with peaches, and why not add a few cups of iced black tea? Instead of juices, you can use various soft drinks, and you can vary the strength and intensity by increasing or decreasing the amount of brandy. Brandy can also be excluded altogether or replaced with vodka.*

The word Sangria comes from 'sangre', the Spanish word for blood, probably because of the blood-red colour of this popular party punch. It is the perfect drink for a summer social. It is deliciously refreshing, but be careful – it is a lot stronger than the sweet taste leads you to believe...

Scarlett O'Hara

2 oz (60 ml) Southern Comfort
½ oz (15 ml) lime juice
Cranberry juice

Pour the Southern Comfort and lime juice into an ice-filled highball glass. Fill up with cranberry juice and stir. Garnish with a strawberry.

TIP! *Why not try Scarlett's partner, Rhett Butler too? Mix 1 ½ oz Southern Comfort, ½ oz orange curaçao, 1 dash lime juice, 1 dash lemon juice and add a lemon twist.*

A long drink from the American South containing its pride among distillates – Southern Comfort.

Screwdriver

2 oz (60 ml) vodka
Orange juice
Orange wedge for garnish

Pour the vodka into an ice-filled highball glass. Fill up with orange juice and garnish with an orange wedge.

TIP! *Add ½ oz Galliano and you have a Harvey Wallbanger!*

Legend has it that an American oil-driller who was working in Iran in the 1950s secretly poured vodka in his thirst-quenching orange juice. He didn't have a spoon to stir with, so he used a screwdriver instead.

Sea Breeze

2 oz (60 ml) vodka
2 oz (60 ml) grapefruit juice
2 oz (60 ml) cranberry juice

Pour all the ingredients into a shaker filled with ice. Shake well and strain into an ice-filled highball glass.

TIP! *Replace the grapefruit juice with pineapple juice to make a sweeter version called Bay Breeze. Or omit the vodka for a refreshing non-alcoholic drink.*

This long drink has always been sensitive to trends – Sea Breeze has had many different guises over the years. In the 1930s it contained gin, apricot brandy and lemon juice, and during the dieting mania of the 1980s, grapefruit juice replaced the apricot brandy. Vodka is the modern gin, and cranberry juice has become immensely popular recently. Remember to shake vigorously to put the froth into the sea breeze.

Sex on the Beach

1 oz (30 ml) vodka
1 oz (30 ml) peach liqueur
Orange juice and cranberry
  juice

Pour the vodka and liqueur
into an ice-filled highball glass.
Fill up with equal parts orange
juice and cranberry juice and
stir.

A beach drink with clear intentions...

Shady Lady

1 oz (30 ml) tequila
1 oz (30 ml) melon liqueur
Grapefruit juice

Pour the tequila and liqueur into an ice-filled highball glass. Fill up with grapefruit juice and stir.

'Shady Lady' with Ani Lorak was Ukraine's contribution in the Eurovision Song Contest 2008 in Belgrade, Serbia. It ended up in second place.

Shandy

Lager
Ginger ale

Pour equal parts lager and
ginger ale into a highball glass
and stir gently.

TIP! *This is the British original
version, although the ginger ale is
sometimes replaced with lemonade,
especially in Europe.*

*Shandy is a famous hangover remedy in England. Beware of ready-made Shandy sold in tins, though.
It normally contains only a fraction of lager and rarely tastes anything like the original.*

Spritzer

3 oz (90 ml) white wine
Sprite

Pour white wine into a large
ice-filled wine glass. Fill up
with Sprite and stir. Garnish
with grapes.

*The world's simplest cocktail? Do you have a friend who tends to stay away from cocktails
and stubbornly sticks to wine at parties? Then this could be a tasty variation.
It's very refreshing and party-like in all its simplicity.*

Summer Princess

2 oz (60 ml) Pisang Ambon
2 oz (60 ml) Licor 43
Milk

Pour the first two ingredients
into an ice-filled highball glass.
Fill up with milk and stir.

*Licor 43 tastes of herbs and vanilla
– just like summer...*

Singapore Sling

1 oz (30 ml) gin
½ oz (15 ml) cherry brandy
½ oz (15 ml) Cointreau
½ oz (15 ml) DOM
  Bénédictine
1 oz (30 ml) lemon juice
½ oz (15 ml) grenadine
½ oz (15 ml) Angostura Bitter
Pineapple juice

Pour the first seven
ingredients into a shaker filled
with ice. Shake well and strain
into an ice-filled highball glass.
Fill up with pineapple juice
and stir.

A 'sling' was originally a long drink made with one spirit, sugar and water only. Liqueur, lemon juice and mixers were added later. Singapore Sling was one of the first cocktails that were considered appropriate for women. It was created in 1915 at the legendary Raffles Hotel in Singapore. Read more about Singapore Sling and the Raffles Hotel in the section about famous cocktail bars.

Smurf

1 oz (30 ml) strawberry vodka
1 oz (30 ml) blue curaçao
Sprite
Lime for garnish

Pour the vodka and curaçao
into an ice-filled highball glass.
Fill up with Sprite and stir.
Garnish with a lime wheel.

The Smurfs sometimes enjoy other drinks than sarsaparilla juice...

Studio 54

1 ½ oz (45 ml) gin
½ oz (15 ml) melon liqueur
Tonic water

Pour the gin and liqueur into an ice-filled highball glass. Fill up with tonic and stir.

Studio 54 was a legendary night club in New York, which had its heyday during the disco era of the 1970s and 80s. The club, which was known as 'The Studio', was so hot that even celebrities had trouble getting past the bouncer …

Tequila Sunrise

2 oz (60 ml) tequila
3 oz (90 ml) orange juice
½ oz (15 ml) grenadine
Orange for garnish

Pour the tequila into an ice-filled highball glass. Fill up with orange juice and stir. Add grenadine carefully, drop by drop, to create a decorative sunset effect. Garnish with a slice of orange and a parasol for a classic, kitschy Sunrise look!

TIP! If you have problems with your sunset, pour grenadine over the back of a teaspoon held close to the edge of the glass.

It's hardly surprising that the famous long drink Tequila Sunrise originated in Mexico, the homeland of tequila. The recipe was first created in the 1930s, but the major breakthrough did not occur until the 1970s, when the Eagles hit single with the same name was released. The sudden success could also have something to do with the film Tequila Sunrise starring Michelle Pfeiffer and Mel Gibson, which was also released around this time.

Vanilla Currant

1 oz (30 ml) vanilla vodka
1 oz (30 ml) Crème de Cassis
1 oz (30 ml) lime juice
Sprite
Fresh blackcurrants for garnish

Fill a glass with crushed ice
and fresh blackcurrants. Add
the vodka, liqueur and lime
juice and stir gently. Fill up
with Sprite and garnish with
blackcurrants.

*Together with the drinking chocolate of the Aztecs, vanilla travelled first to Spain, and from there
it spread to the rest of Europe. In 1602, Elizabeth I's apothecary discovered that vanilla was a
perfect flavour enhancer for sweets, but it would take another 100 years before vanilla had its real
breakthrough in Europe for a completely different reason, its reputation as potency enhancer...*

Wolf's Paw

2 oz (60 ml) vodka
Lingonberry juice

Pour the vodka into an
ice-filled highball glass. Fill
up with lingonberry juice
and stir. Garnish with fresh
lingonberries or cranberries.

TIP! *Lingonberries are a
Scandinavian delicacy that may be
hard to come by. Luckily, they can
be easily substituted by cranberries.*

*This recipe comes from the so-called Vodka Belt of northern Scandinavia. The original recipe goes as
follows: 'Pour vodka into a glass. Quickly dip a lingonberry into the vodka. Knock back!'*

Vanilla Sky

1 oz (30 ml) vanilla vodka
1 oz (30 ml) pineapple liqueur
1 oz (30 ml) lime juice
Lemonade

Pour the first three ingredients into an ice-filled highball glass. Fill up with lemonade and stir.

This long drink was first launched at the opening night of the film Vanilla Sky, starring Tom Cruise and Penelope Cruz.

Zombie

1 oz (30 ml) light rum
1 oz (30 ml) dark rum
1 oz (30 ml) Jamaican rum
½ oz (15 ml) Cointreau
½ oz (15 ml) apricot brandy
½ oz (15 ml) lime juice
½ oz (15 ml) grenadine
Pineapple juice

Pour all ingredients except the pineapple juice into a shaker filled with ice. Shake vigorously and strain into a huge ice-filled highball glass. Fill up with pineapple juice and pass it to a friend...

TIP! Beware. The strength of a Zombie made according to the original recipe is equal to 3.5 normal cocktails. Although this version is not quite that bad, don't let your friend drink more than one unless you want him or her to feel like a zombie the next morning...

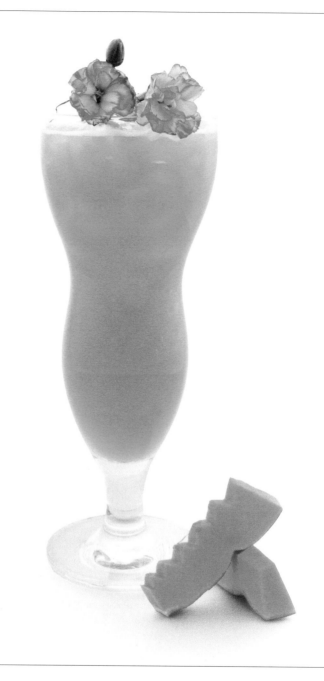

Restaurateur Don Beach created this recipe in 1934. After having been made aware of the effects, he introduced a limit of maximum two Zombies per person and night. Which added up to about 7 normal drinks...

Winter Kiss

1 oz (30 ml) whisky,
  preferably bourbon
1 oz (30 ml) raspberry liqueur
10 fresh raspberries
1 oz (30 ml) lemon juice
½ oz (15 ml) simple syrup
Splash of lemonade

Muddle most of the raspberries with the lemon juice and syrup in a shaker. Add ice cubes, the whisky and the liqueur. Shake well and strain into a highball glass. Fill up with crushed ice and top with lemonade. Garnish with fresh raspberries.

*This refreshing long drink is excellent after a heavy meal,
and is the perfect finale to a Christmas dinner.*

Hot Drinks and After-Dinner Cocktails

What is better than snuggling up by the fire on a cold winter's day with a warm drink? Or enjoying one after a meal instead of dessert – it is like having coffee, liqueur and a piece of cake all in one go! Coffee lovers rejoice over having their favourite drink turned into a party cocktail, and there are many hot chocolate drinks to try out for those nostalgic people who are past their teens .

THE HEAT TRICK

Hot drinks should always be served in a heatproof glass with a stem or a handle for holding it. Put a spoon in the glass to prevent it from cracking when you pour in the hot liquid – the metal conducts the heat. This is especially important if you are using a heat sensitive glass such as a wine glass. Prepare it by filling it with hot water before preparing the drink.

THE CREAM FLOAT

Many hot drinks have a 'cream lid' that floats elegantly on the surface without blending with the rest of the drink. Bartenders usually achieve this by gently pouring the cream over the back of a spoon held close to the edge of the glass. To succeed, the cream should not be whipped too hard. It should still be a little runny or it will clot and sink.

Sprinkling some additional seasoning over the cream on top of a hot coffee or a chocolate drinkis is not necessary, but delicious! Try cinnamon, cardamom, nutmeg, cocoa powder or grated chocolate.

French Coffee

2 oz (60 ml) Cointreau
Hot coffee
Orange peel
Lightly whipped cream

Add a little grated orange peel to the cream before whipping it. Pour Cointreau into a heatproof glass and fill up with coffee. Float the cream on top.

TIP! *Place a teaspoon in the glass before adding the hot coffee – it will prevent it from cracking.*

A French Coffee using Grand Marnier instead of Cointreau is called a Café Parisienne.
Use the Mandarine Napoléon liqueur, and you have made a Café Imperial.

Après-Ski Choc

2 oz (60 ml) gold rum or dark
  rum
5 oz (150 ml) milk
1 tbsp cocoa powder
Lightly whipped cream

Heat up milk, cocoa powder
and rum in a saucepan. Whip
until slightly frothy and pour
into a heatproof glass. Float
the cream on top.

TIP! *Are you finding it hard to
make the cream float? Use a trick
of the trade: pour the cream gently
over the back of a teaspoon.*

This is an Irish coffee for those who love rum but not coffee!

Amaretto Coffee

2 oz (60 ml) amaretto
Hot coffee
Lightly whipped cream

Pour the amaretto into a heatproof glass. Fill up with coffee and float cream on top according to the instructions on page 264.

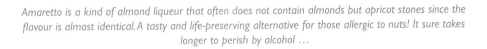

Amaretto is a kind of almond liqueur that often does not contain almonds but apricot stones since the flavour is almost identical. A tasty and life-preserving alternative for those allergic to nuts! It sure takes longer to perish by alcohol …

Anatole Coffee

1 oz (30 ml) Frangelico
½ oz (15 ml) brandy
½ oz (15 ml) Kahlúa
Cold coffee
Lightly whipped cream

Pour the brandy and liqueurs into a shaker filled with ice. Shake well and strain into any glass. Fill up with coffee and float cream on top according to the instructions on page 264.

Anatolia is a peninsula in West Asia that makes up most of Turkey. The most important city today is Ankara, the capital of Turkey, which is situated at the centre of the peninsula. The historical city of Troy was once situated in Anatolia. Anatolia means sunrise, but at that time of day a regular cup of coffee might be preferable...

Baileys Coffee

2 oz (60 ml) Baileys
Hot coffee
Lightly whipped cream

Pour the Baileys into a heatproof glass. Fill up with coffee and float cream on top according to the instructions on page 264.

TIP! *Place a teaspoon in the glass before adding the hot coffee to prevent the glass from cracking.*

Baileys, one of the world's best-known liqueurs, is based on cream and whisky. It was launched in Ireland in the 1970s and soon became so successful that Ireland had to start importing dairy products — half the domestic milk production was used for producing Baileys for export ...

Irish Coffee

2 oz (60 ml) Irish whiskey
1–2 tsp brown sugar
Hot coffee
Lightly whipped cream

Pour the sugar and a little
hot coffee into a heatproof
glass. Stir until the sugar
dissolves. Add whiskey and
fill up with more coffee. Float
cream on top according to
the instructions on page
264. NB: The brown sugar
is essential for the cream to
float properly.

TIP! *In general, hot coffee drinks,
including Irish Coffee, are rarely
served with a straw, nor stirred. The
hot coffee should be enjoyed filtered
through the cold cream.*

*The origin of Irish Coffee is greatly disputed. According to certain sources, the original Irish coffee was
invented by Joseph Sheridan, head chef at Shannon Airport in western Ireland. The recipe was conceived
after a group of American passengers had disembarked there on a miserable winter evening in the
1940s. To warm the passengers, Sheridan combined the Irish tradition of adding whiskey to their tea
with the American love for coffee. It was a given success.*

Cuban Coffee

1 ½ oz (45 ml) dark rum
½ oz (15 ml) dark Crème de
  Cacao
Hot coffee
Lightly whipped cream

Pour the rum and liqueur in
a heatproof glass. Fill up with
coffee and float cream on top
according to the instructions
on page 264.

TIP! *Try sprinkling cinnamon,
cardamom, nutmeg, cocoa powder
or grated chocolate on the cream.
Yummy!*

*Mojito, Daiquiri and Cuba Libre are Cuba's three national drinks, in that order. They are all
based on light or dark rum and lime juice. Lime is not included Cuban Coffee, however...*

Jamaican Coffee

2 oz (60 ml) dark rum,
preferably Jamaican
1 tsp demerara sugar
Hot coffee
Lightly whipped cream

Pour the sugar and coffee into
a heatproof glass. Stir to make
the sugar dissolve. Add rum and
fill up with more coffee. Float
cream on top according to the
instructions on page 264.

TIP! *Place a teaspoon in the glass
before adding the hot coffee. The
metal in the spoon will conduct
away the heat, which prevents the
glass from cracking.*

*This is an international version of the classic after-dinner delight Irish Coffee. The Irish whiskey
of the original has been exchanged for rum for a more Jamaican flavour.*

Mint Chocolate Coffee

2 oz (60 ml) Baileys Mint
  Chocolate
Hot coffee, preferably espresso
Hot milk
Mint leaf for garnish

Pour the liqueur into a
heatproof glass and fill up
with equal parts milk and
coffee. Top with milk froth and
garnish with a mint leaf.

TIP! *For a non-alcoholic version,
replace the liqueur with mint syrup.*

*An After Eight mint chocolate in liquid
form to enjoy after a sturdy meal.*

Mexican Coffee

2 oz (60 ml) Kahlúa
1 tsp demerara sugar
Hot coffee
Lightly whipped cream

Pour the sugar and coffee into
a heatproof glass. Stir to make
the sugar dissolve. Add Kahlúa
and fill up with more coffee.
Float cream on top according
to the instructions on page 264.

If you want an even more Mexican touch to your coffee,
use 1 oz Kahlúa and 1 oz tequila instead.

Winter's Night

2 oz (60 ml) pear brandy
Hot chocolate
Lightly whipped cream

Pour the liqueur into a heatproof glass. Fill up with coffee and float cream on top according to the instructions on page 264.

Pear brandy is usually made with Williams pears, or Bartlett pears as they are called in the U.S. and Canada. For this reason, the brandy is often simply called Poire Williams.

Irish Traitor

2 oz (60 ml) Drambuie
Hot coffee
Lightly whipped cream

Pour the liqueur into a heatproof glass. Fill up with coffee and float cream on top according to the instructions on page 264.

TIP! *Skip the straw – enjoy the coffee through the cold cream float.*

Many choose to add liqueur in their Irish coffee rather than the whiskey of the original. These drinks are humorously called Irish Traitors.

Tiramisù Ice Coffee

1 oz (30 ml) coffee liqueur
½ oz (15 ml) Marsala wine
½ oz (15 ml) white Crème de Cacao
2 tbsp mascarpone cheese
1 oz (30 ml) single cream
Lightly whipped cream

Pour the coffee liqueur into a coffee mug. Pour Marsala wine, Crème de Cacao and mascarpone cheese into a shaker filled with ice. Shake vigorously and strain into the mug. Float cream on top according to the instructions on page 264.

A cream come true? This Italian world-famous national dessert is a favourite of many – and here you find it in an irresistible liquid version! The name literally means 'pick me up' which, refers to the coffee and chocolate, both of which are rich in caffeine.

Lumumba

2 oz (60 ml) brandy
Hot chocolate
Lightly whipped cream

Pour the brandy into a
heatproof glass. Fill up with
hot chocolate and float cream
on top according to the
instructions on page 264.

TIP! *Lumumba is delicious served
cold too, in a highball glass with ice
cubes.*

*Brandy is a distilled spirit made from fruit juice. Cognac, the best known variety, has originates from the
Cognac district in south-western France. Since brandy was able to survive the long transport without any
negative effects on the quality, it quickly became popular throughout Europe, particularly in Holland.*

Liquid Cocaine

1 oz (30 ml) lemon vodka
1 oz (30 ml) Kahlúa
½ oz (15 ml) simple syrup
1 oz (30 ml) cold espresso
Lemon twist for garnish

Brew the espresso and leave
to cool. Pour the other
ingredients into a shaker filled
with ice. Shake well and strain
into a chilled cocktail glass.
Twist a lemon peel over the
drink to release a drop of oil
and use the peel for garnish.

This is how to spell afternoon tea when you are on holiday!
It's incredibly addictive …

Chocolate Martini

1 oz (30 ml) vodka
½ oz (15 ml) Crème de Cacao
½ oz (15 ml) Frangelico

Pour all the ingredients into
a shaker filled with ice. Shake
well and strain into a chilled
cocktail glass.

*Gin plays the leading part in one of the world's most famous cocktails: Dry Martini. This immortal
classic has been around since at least 1862, when it appeared in the book The Bartender's Guide – the
First Comprehensive Manual for Bartenders. However, many believe that the recipe was created as
early as in the 1820s. Today, there are hundreds of Martinis, many made with vodka rather than gin.*

Brandy Alexander

1 oz (30 ml) brandy
1 oz (30 ml) dark Crème de Cacao
1 oz (30 ml) double cream
Cocoa powder or nutmeg for garnish

Pour the ingredients into a shaker filled with ice. Shake well and strain into a chilled cocktail glass. Dust some cocoa powder or nutmeg on top.

The original Alexander from the 1920s contains gin, but Brandy Alexander is without doubt the more famous version of this after dinner treat.

Piña Colada

2 oz (60 ml) light rum
2 oz (60 ml) thick coconut milk
3 oz (90 ml) pineapple juice
Crushed ice

Pour all the ingredients into an electric blender. Blend briefly at high speed until smooth. Pour into an exotic hurricane glass and garnish with a tropical touch.

TIP! *For a thicker Colada, use fresh crushed pineapple instead of juice. Use cream and coconut syrup if you cannot get hold of coconut milk.*

There is a reason why this flavour combination is known all over the world as a classic; however, the original recipe contained no coconut milk at all. The drink's name literally means crushed pineapple.

Banana Colada

1 oz (30 ml) light rum
1 oz (30 ml) dark rum
2 oz (60 ml) thick coconut milk
3 oz (90 ml) pineapple juice
½ banana
Crushed ice

Pour all the ingredients into a blender. Blend briefly at high speed until smooth. Pour into an exotic hurricane glass and garnish with banana.

TIP! *Piña Colada was originally made with crushed pineapple and crushed ice, with a consistency similar to sorbet. The 'frozenness' of your Colada is completely optional, add the ice a little at a time until you are satisfied with the texture.*

Use Midori liqueur instead of a banana to mix yourself a Midori Colada.
Pear brandy makes a Pear Colada, and so on...

Kiwi Colada

1 ½ oz (45 ml) white rum
½ oz (15 ml) melon liqueur
½ oz (15 ml) thick coconut
  milk
2 oz (60 ml) pineapple juice
½ oz (15 ml) double cream
1 kiwi, save some for garnish
Crushed ice

Pour the ingredients into a
blender. Blend briefly at high
speed until smooth. Pour into
an exotic hurricane glass and
garnish with kiwi.

If you wash the kiwi carefully, you can eat the skin.
It is soft, rich in flavour and nutritious.

Strawberry Colada

1 ½ oz (45 ml) white rum
½ oz (15 ml) strawberry
 liqueur
½ oz (45 ml) thick coconut
 milk
2 oz (60 ml) pineapple juice
½ oz (15 ml) double cream
4 strawberries + 1 for garnish
Crushed ice

Pour the ingredients into a
blender. Blend briefly at high
speed until smooth. Pour
into an exotic hurricane
glass and garnish with fresh
strawberries.

*In general, women have more taste buds on their tongues than men, which normally makes them more
sensitive to strong and intense flavours. The difference can be enormous – one person can have 11 taste
buds per square centimetre and someone else 1,100! There are, of course, individual differences, but this
could be a reason why women are often prone to liking sweet and fruity 'girly drinks' such as this...*

Pink Panther

1 oz (30 ml) vodka
1 oz (30 ml) amaretto
2 dashes grenadine
2 oz (60 ml) double cream

Pour the ingredients into a
shaker filled with ice. Shake
well and strain into an ice-
filled highball glass.

*The Pink Panther character is associated with a number of cancer awareness and support
organisations. It is the mascot of the New Zealand Child Cancer foundation as well as of a line of
clothing which promotes breast cancer awareness.*

BMW

⅔ oz (20 ml) Baileys
⅔ oz (20 ml) Malibu
⅔ oz (20 ml) whisky

Pour the ingredients into a shaker filled with ice. Shake well and strain into an ice-filled tumbler.

Drinking and driving is never okay, not even when it comes to a drink with this name …

Godchild

1 ½ oz (45 ml)
½ oz (15 ml) amaretto
1 oz (30 ml) double cream

Pour the ingredients into a
shaker filled with ice. Shake
well and strain into an ice-
filled tumbler.

*For those who feel that alcohol and children do not belong together, there is a non-alcoholic version
with the same name that contains Sprite, 1 oz blackcurrant juice and a dash of lemon juice.*

Golden Cadillac

1 oz (30 ml) Galliano
1 oz (30 ml) white Crème de Cacao
1 oz (30 ml) double cream

Pour the ingredients into a shaker filled with ice. Shake well and strain into a chilled cocktail glass.

TIP! *Try replacing the Crème de Cacao with 1 oz orange juice and 1 oz Cointreau and decrease the amount of cream. Ta daa! You have made yourself a Golden Dream.*

This is a cocktail with a shade of gold – creamy and luxurious. The name Golden Cadillac is only natural. If you fancy even more luxury, add a scoop of vanilla ice-cream.

KGB

²/₃ oz (20 ml) Kahlúa
²/₃ oz (20 ml) Grand Marnier
  Rouge
²/₃ oz (20 ml) Baileys

Pour the ingredients into a
shaker filled with ice. Shake
well and strain into a chilled
cocktail glass. Sprinkle some
grated chocolate on top.

TIP! *If the abbreviation KGB gives
you the creeps, why not settle for a
GB or a KB?*

*The KGB was the national security organisation of the Soviet Union between 1954 and 1991. Their
members often recruited neighbours and relatives as informants in pursuit of regime critics. This
cocktail is so delicious that you will do just about anything to get a taste, but the KGB probably used
very different methods.*

Grasshopper

1 oz (30 ml) white Crème de Cacao
1 oz (30 ml) green Crème de Menthe
1 oz (30 ml) double cream
Chocolate shavings for garnish

Pour the ingredients into a shaker filled with ice. Shake well and strain into a chilled cocktail glass. Sprinkle some grated chocolate on top.

TIP! *Replace the cream with vodka to make a Flying Grasshopper!*

It was surely not this type of grasshopper that God sent as a punishment to the people of Egypt in the biblical story — this delicious dream of a cocktail can hardly be considered a pest.

Pisang Pistachio

1 ½ oz (45 ml) Pisang Ambon
½ oz (15 ml) amaretto
1 ox (30 ml) double cream

Pour the ingredients into a
shaker filled with ice. Shake
well and strain into a chilled
cocktail glass.

TIP! *You can replace the cream
with milk.*

*Pisang Ambon is a bright green, ancient Indonesian liqueur manufactured by the Dutch company Bols.
Bols is the largest distillery in the world. It was established by Lucas Bols as early as in 1575. Some of
the liqueurs from that time are manufactured to this day, such as blue curaçao and Parfait Amour.*

Milky Valentine

1 oz (30 ml) strawberry liqueur
½ oz (15 ml) Baileys
½ oz (15 ml) Kahlúa
2 oz (60 ml) milk

Pour the ingredients into a shaker filled with ice. Shake well and strain into a tumbler. Fill up with crushed ice and serve with a straw.

Many girls may prefer their box of chocolate in liquid form on Valentine's Day, and perhaps many boys too …

Orgasm

1 oz (30 ml) Baileys
½ oz (15 ml) Kahlúa
½ oz (15 ml) amaretto
2 oz (60 ml) milk

Pour the ingredients into a shaker filled with ice. Shake well and strain into an ice-filled highball glass.

TIP! *Guests tend to ask about the name of the drink they've just been served. If you feel that you have to lie to grandma – serve something else instead …*

'Well, sure, just let me finish my shift first,' the confused newly-employed bartender replied when a girl asked for the milkshake-tasting long drink with the shameless name …

Screaming Orgasm

½ oz (15 ml) vodka
1 oz (30 ml) Baileys
½ oz (15 ml) Kahlúa

Fill a tumbler with crushed ice. Add all the ingredients and stir gently.

TIP! *Be sure to use high-quality vodka. Cheap vodka may cause the Baileys to curdle. Test the vodka by mixing a teaspoon with a little Baileys before making the drink.*

Will have you screaming for more …

Silk Stockings

1 ½ oz (45 ml) white tequila
½ oz (15 ml) white Crème de
 Cacao
1 oz (30 ml) single cream
1 dash grenadine

Pour the ingredients into a
shaker filled with ice. Shake
well and strain into a chilled
cocktail glass.

TIP! *Try sprinkling some cinnamon
on top and serve it by the bedside
with chocolate truffles.*

*Silk Stockings is a musical by Cole Porter. In 1957, it was made into a film starring Fred Astaire and
dancer Cyd Charisse – the lady with the fantastic legs who also dances with Gene Kelly in Singin' in the
Rain. Could the name of this cocktail be an allusion to her? Nobody knows...*

Silk Stockings Valentine

1 oz (30 ml) tequila
½ oz (15 ml) white Crème de Cacao
½ oz (15 ml) strawberry liqueur
Grated chocolate for garnish

Pour the ingredients into a shaker filled with ice. Shake well and strain into a chilled cocktail glass. Garnish with a chocolate rim.

Chocolate rim: Pour grated chocolate onto a saucer. Moisten the rim of the glass with a little simple syrup and dip the upturned glass into the chocolate.

Just when you thought it couldn't get any more romantic, these pink silk stockings appear. This sassy after-dinner cocktail can make anyone lose their head...

White Russian

1 ½ oz (45 ml) vodka
½ oz (15 ml) Kahlúa
1 oz (30 ml) milk

Pour the ingredients into a shaker filled with ice. Shake well and strain into an ice-filled tumbler.

TIP! *It has been highly disputed whether this timeless drink should contain equal parts vodka and Kahlúa or a greater proportion of vodka, as above. Some people prefer cream instead of milk.*

This drink plays an important supporting role in the film The Big Lebowski. It has a big brother named Black Russian, and in some parts of the world, a White Russian is simply a Black Russian topped with a little whipped cream.

Vanilla White Russian

1 ½ oz (45 ml) vanilla vodka
½ oz (15 ml) Kahlúa
1 oz (30 ml) milk
Lightly whipped cream

Pour the ingredients into a shaker filled with ice. Shake well and strain into an ice-filled tumbler. Float a little cream on top.

According to some studies, men and women experience flavours in different ways. Also, men tend to choose stronger beverages while women are attracted by milder and sweeter drinks in which the bitter flavours of the spirit are disguised. White Russian is traditionally considered a 'girly' drink.

Non-Alcoholic Cocktails

'A man who drinks only water has a secret to hide from his fellow men.'

Charles Baudelaire 1821–1867

We couldn't agree less with the quote above. Life is a party, and there is always an opportunity to celebrate something in the company of good friends even though you may not always feel like – or be able to – drink alcohol. Today, with the aid of syrups and other flavourings, most cocktails can be made in a non-alcoholic version. If it is the flavour of a specific cocktail you're after, but don't fancy getting tipsy, you have nothing to worry about.

But what about getting drunk and the sense of freedom and relaxation? Well, rumour has it that part of it is all in your head anyway. In fact, it can be enough just to be in the same room as intoxicated people to feel a little giddy. It has been scientifically proven that intoxication is 'contagious' to a certain degree – it causes people to act as if they are more drunk than they really are. Humans are flock animals; if the flock is having fun and is acting intoxicated we all feel a little drunk. Nobody can possibly know who started it.

If you enjoy non-alcoholic cocktails every now and then (or always) there are a couple of additional advantages: you won't end up spending as much money as your boozing friends, and you won't have to nurse a hangover the next day. So keep it up! No matter if your reasons are to do with health, lifestyle or pregnancy, there is no reason to miss out on all the fun. In this chapter, you will find some delicious mocktails for the times when you want to pass on the booze but not on the party!

Shirley Temple

1 oz (30 ml) grenadine
Ginger ale
Orange slice and maraschino
  cherry for garnish

Pour the grenadine into an
ice-filled highball glass and fill
up with ginger ale. Garnish
with an orange slice and a
maraschino cherry.

TIP! *The original was made with
lemonade, so if you really want to
feel like a child in the 1930s, use
Sprite instead.*

*The most successful American child movie star of all time was born in 1928. She used to go to galas
and film premières all the time but was of course not allowed to drink alcohol. This mocktail was
created especially for her. Shirley Temple later became a politician and a diplomat.*

Mint Apple Lemonade

1 oz (30 ml) lemon juice
½ oz (15 ml) simple syrup
6 mint leaves
Diced apple
Lemonade
2 lemon wedges and lemon
  wheel for garnish

Muddle the mint leaves and
a few apple dices together
with syrup in a highball glass.
Fill up with ice cubes, diced
apple and lemon wedges. Add
lemon juice and fill up with
lemonade. Garnish with a
lemon wheel.

*A muddler is for the bartender what a mortar is for the chef. When muddling mint leaves,
the delicious spicy mint oil is released and adds a kick to this lovely summer drink!*

Strawberry Juice

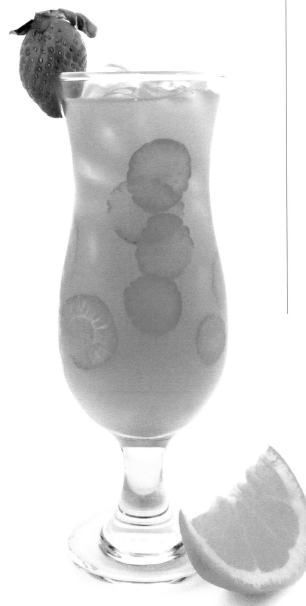

1 oz (30 ml) orange juice
1 oz (30 ml) grapefruit juice
½ oz (15 ml) lemon juice
½ oz (15 ml) simple syrup
4–5 fresh strawberries, save
  one for garnish
1 pinch salt

Slice the strawberries and place half of them in a highball glass. Add the lemon juice, syrup and salt and stir gently. Add ice cubes and the rest of the strawberries until the glass is half-full. Pour in the orange juice and grapefruit juice. Garnish with a strawberry.

Grapefruit juice is sometimes used in aromatherapy as grapefruit peel contains a substance that is believed to produce euphoria.

Virgin Piña Colada

4 oz (120 ml) pineapple juice
1 ½ oz (45 ml) thick coconut
  milk
Crushed ice
Pineapple wedge for garnish

Pour the ingredients into an
electric blender. Blend briefly
at high speed. Start with a
small amount of crushed ice
and add more until you get
the right consistency. Pour
into an exotic Hurricane glass
and garnish with a pineapple
wedge.

TIP! *For a more intense flavour
– exchange the coconut milk for a
spoonful of whipped cream mixed
with coconut syrup.*

*Piña Colada is probably the best known beach drink of all, and many bartenders have claimed its
classic combination of flavours as their own invention. Piña Colada literally means 'crushed pineapple'
and this version suits anyone who is a big pineapple lover but can do without the rum of the original.*

Virgin Strawberry Colada

3 oz (90 ml) pineapple juice
1 ½ oz (45 ml) thick coconut
  milk
5 fresh strawberries
Crushed ice

Pour the ingredients into an electric blender. Blend briefly at high speed and pour into an exotic glass.

TIP! *For a more intense strawberry flavour – add 1–2 tsp strawberry syrup.*

This Colada combines sweet strawberries from your garden and a tropical holiday paradise …

Witch's Brew

1 dash grenadine
3 dashes blue curaçao syrup
Lemonade

Add the grenadine to a small
glass of your choice and fill up
with ice cubes. Add curaçao
syrup in drops and fill up
with lemonade. Play around
with the syrups to create the
colour effect you prefer!

TIP! *Garnish with scary Halloween
decorations such as bats, spiders
and worms. Romantic witches
choose flowers instead …*

*This is a suitable drink for all witches, ghosts
and monsters at the Halloween party.*

Virgin Strawberry Daiquiri

3 oz (90 ml) strawberries
½ oz (15 ml) strawberry syrup
1 oz (30 ml) lime juice
Crushed ice

TIP! *Add the ice a little at a time and stop when you have the right consistency.*

A Daiquiri that may not have been appreciated by 'Papa Double' …

Virgin Frozen Ruby Red

2 oz (60 ml) Tropicana Ruby
  Breakfast
2 dashes grenadine
Crushed ice

Pour the ingredients into an
electric blender. Blend briefly
at high speed. Start with a
small amount of crushed ice
and add more until you have
the right consistency.

TIP! *You can skip the blender
and pour the drink in an ice-filled
highball glass instead if you like.*

*This is a perfect aperitif if stirred with ice cubes, or a refreshing beach drink if frozen – it's up to
you. Ruby is a type of blood grapefruit. The tanginess of the grapefruit balances the sweetness of the
grenadine perfectly and makes this drink a refreshing, alcohol-free treat.*

Safe Sex on the Beach

1 ½ oz (45 ml) peach nectar
2 oz (60 ml) cranberry juice
2 oz (60 ml) pineapple juice
Mixed fruit for garnish

Fill up a highball glass with
fruit and ice cubes. Add the
juices and stir gently.

TIP! *If you want a flavour that is
closer to the original, use orange
juice instead of pineapple juice.*

*Nectar was the favoured, aromatic drink of the Olympic gods. It was believed to offer eternal youth and
immortality. Alcoholic cocktails can produce the same (imagined) effect. With an alcohol-free drink, you'll
keep both feet on the ground …*

Virgin Vanilla Currant

1 oz (30 ml) blackcurrant cordial
½ oz (15 ml) vanilla syrup
Grape tonic
3 oz (90 ml) blackcurrants

Muddle the blackcurrants with vanilla syrup in a highball glass. Add the blackcurrant cordial and crushed ice. Fill up with grape tonic.

Syrups can in most cases replace liqueurs in an alcohol-free drink. There are uncountable variations of different-flavoured syrups that can be bought in supermarkets and drink shops.

True Long Island Iced Tea

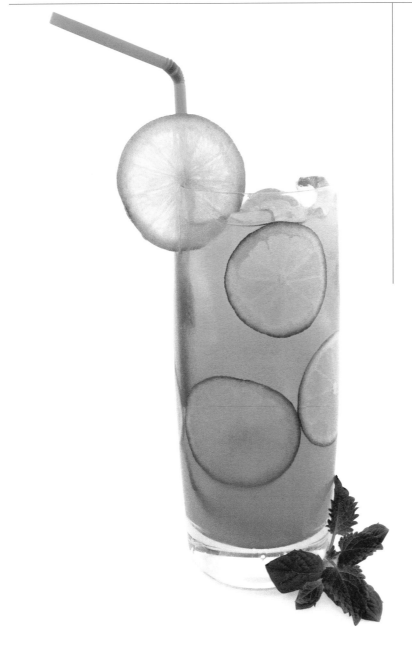

1 ½ oz (45 ml) peach iced tea
1 ½ oz (45 ml) non-alcoholic
  apple cider
1 ½ oz (45 ml) lemon juice
Ginger ale
Lime slices for garnish

Pour the ingredients except
the ginger ale into an ice-filled
highball glass. Fill up with
ginger ale and stir. Garnish
with lime slices.

TIP! *If you want a more traditional
Long Island flavour, replace the
ginger ale with coke.*

A little closer to the truth than the original …

Index

Spirit Index

RUM DRINKS

Alaska Iced Tea	216
Apple Mojito	233
Après-Ski Choc	266
Bahama Mama	183
Banana Colada	283
Bangkok Iced Tea	217
Beverly Hills Iced Tea	218
Blackcurrant Caipirinha	136
Blue Hawaiian	188
Caipirinha	134
Caribbean Madras	229
Chill Out	191
Collins	196
Coriander & Chilli	95
Cuba Libre	203
Cuban Coffee	271
Enok	201
Fidel Castro	202
Frozen Banana Daiquiri	147
Frozen Blackberry Daiquiri	145
Frozen Blueberry Daiquiri	146
Frozen Daiquiri	144
Frozen Mango Daiquiri	149
Frozen Mojito	143
Frozen Peach Daiquiri	150
Frozen Raspberry Daiquiri	151
Frozen Strawberry Daiquiri	148
Ginger Kumquat Caipirinha	135
Happy Medium	69
Havana Hot Nights	213
Hemingway Special	120
Indo	215
Jamaican Coffee	272
Kiwi Colada	284
Long Beach Iced Tea	221
Long Island Iced Tea	222
Mai Tai	231
Mango Lemonade	227
Mojito	232
Nacional de Cuba	121
Orange Mojito	234
Palm Beach	74
Piña Colada	282
Pomegranate Mojito	235
Strawberry Colada	285
Thai Mojito	236
Tropical Caipirinha	134
Zombie	262

BRANDY DRINKS

Between The Sheets	65
Black Cat	184
Brandy Alexander	281
Brandy Sour	130
Collins	196
French Connection	115
Horse's Neck	214
Lumumba	278
Sidecar	63

WHISKY DRINKS

American Dream	181
Collins	196
Elite	113
Godfather	119
Green Day	68
Green Mist	71
Irish Coffee	270
Irish Iced Tea	219
Lynchburg Lemonade	226
Manhattan	61
Mint Julep	123
New York Sour	133
Old Fashioned	126
Red Baron	72
Rob Roy	62
Rusty Nail	127
Whisky Sour	132
Winter Kiss	263

LIQUEUR DRINKS

Amaretto Coffee	267
Americano	105
Anatole Coffee	268
B-52	165
Baileys Coffee	269
Blow Job	166
BMW	287
Chartreuse and Tonic	193
El Niño	112
French Coffee	265
Frozen Cappuccino	158
Galliano Hot Shot	168
Garden	66
Golden Cadillac	289
Grand Passion	210
Grasshopper	291
Irish Traitor	276
Japanese Slipper	73
KGB	290
Lennart	224
Liquid Viagra	171
Mexican Coffee	274
Milky Valentine	293
Mint Chocolate Coffee	273
Orgasm	294
Paintball	172
Pisang Pistachio	292
Raspberry Kiss	156
Scarlett O'Hara	247
Screaming Orgasm	295
Slippery Nipple	174
St. Patrick's Shooter	175
Stars and Stripes	177
Strawberry Kiss	157
Summer Princess	254
Tiramisù Ice Coffee	277
Winter's Night	275

ABSINTH DRINKS

Blackberry Beast	185

BEER DRINKS

Shandy	252

WINE DRINKS

Absolut Green Wedding	97
Bellini	98
Blackberry Bellini	99
Ferrari	108
Italian Iced Tea	220
Kir Royale	100
My Funny Valentine	96
Ritz Fizz	103
Rossini	102
Sangria	246
Spritzer	253

Liqueurs

LIQUEUR	CONTENTS	FLAVOUR
Advocaat	Brandy, egg yolk, sugar	Egg toddy
Amaretto	Almonds, apricots, spices	Almonds
Amarula	Marula berries, cream	Toffee, vanilla, strawberries
Aniseette	Anisee seed	Liquorice
Apricot brandy	Apricots	Apricots
Baileys	Whisky, cocoa, vanilla, cream	Whisky, milk chocolate, toffee
Baja Rosa	Tequila, strawberries	Strawberry milk
Bénédictine D.O.M	Angelica, hyssop, lemon balm	Herb brandy, honey
Butterscotch	Toffee	Toffee
Campari	Secret Italian recipe	Cough medicine
Chambord	Blackberries, raspberries, currants, strawberries	Raspberries
Chartreuse	More than 100 different herbs	Cough medicine
Cherry Heering	Cherries, herbs	Cherries
Cointreau	Orange peel	Sweet and sour orange
Cherry brandy	Cherries	Cherries
Crème de Bananes	Banana	Banana
Crème de Cacao	Cocoa	Chocolate
Crème de Cassis	Blackcurrants	Blackcurrants, blackberries
Crème de Fraise	Strawberries	Strawberries
Crème de Menthe	Peppermint	Mint
Crème de Mûre	Blackberries	Blackberries
Crème de Noix	Walnuts	Walnuts
Crème de Noisette	Hazelnuts	Hazelnuts
Crème de Noyaux	Peach, plum and cherry stones	Bitter almonds
Crème de Violette	Vanilla, cocoa	Vanilla, chocolate
Curaçao (blue, yellow, red, green)	Bitter orange peel	Oranges
Danziger Goldwasser	Citrus liquor, gold leaf	Cumin, anise seed
Dooley's	Fudge	Toffee
Drambuie	Single malt whisky, herbs, spices	Sweet herbal whisky
Frangelico	Hazelnuts	Hazelnuts

LIQUEUR	CONTENTS	FLAVOUR
Galliano	Herbs and spices e.g. vanilla, anise seed	Sweet and spicy vanilla, anise seed
Gold Strike	24 K gold leaves, cinnamon, cardamom, cloves	Cinnamon
Grand Marnier	Cognac, oranges	Sweet cognac
Kahlúa	Coffee	Coffee
Licor 43	Herbs, vanilla	Herbs, vanilla
Limoncello	Lemon peel	Sweet lemon
Lychee	Lychee	Lychee
Malibu	Coconut	Coconut
Mandarine Napoléon	Brandy, tangerine peel	Tangerine
Maraschino	Bittersweet cherries	Bitter almonds
Midori	Melon	Melon
Parfait Amour	Curaçao with orange peel, vanilla, violet	Citrus, vanilla, violet
Passoã	Passion fruit juice	Passion fruit, blood oranges
Peachtree	Peaches	Citrus, peaches
Pisang Ambon	Green banana	Fruity banana
Punsch	Arrack, water, sugar	Sweet arrack
Sambuca	Anise seed	Liquorice
Sloe Gin	Sloe berries	Sweet and sour sloe berries
Sève Fournier	Vanilla, iris, cocoa beans	Fruity brandy
Strega	Pepper, iris, cinnamon, juniper berries, saffron	Herbs, citrus, toffee, banana
Southern Comfort	Fresh peaches	Bourbon, citrus, apricots
Sourz Apple	Apples	Sweet apples
Sourz Pineapple	Pineapple	Sour pineapple
Tequila Rose	Tequila, strawberries	Strawberry milk
Tia Maria	Coffee	Coffee
Triple Sec	Sweet and sour orange peel	Oranges
Tuaca	Cocoa, egg yolk	Chocolate
Wild Africa	Toffee, vanilla	Toffee, vanilla
Xanté Poire au Cognac	Pears, cognac	Pears, cognac